THE MURDER OF OSCAR CHITWOOD IN HOT SPRINGS, ARKANSAS

THE MURDER OF OSCAR CHITWOOD IN HOT SPRINGS, ARKANSAS

GUY LANCASTER AND CHRISTOPHER THRASHER

Published by The History Press
Charleston, SC
www.historypress.com

First published 2022

Manufactured in the United States

ISBN 9781467153270

Library of Congress Control Number: 2022943528

CONTENTS

ACKNOWLEDGEMENTS

My work is dedicated in loving memory of my mother, Theresa Thrasher (1953–2021).

I am grateful to my coauthor, Guy Lancaster. Guy has a unique talent for bringing out the best in writers. I do not know how he does it, but I know that I am a better writer because he does it.

I thank Liz Robbins and the entire team at the Garland County Historical Society. This book was only possible because of the encouragement, support and guidance of the award-winning Garland County Historical Society.

I appreciate Tom and Mary Hill, at Hot Springs National Park, who taught me most of what I know about Hot Springs, Arkansas.

I am grateful to Abby Hanks for her helpful comments on several portions of this manuscript.

I am thankful for my father, David Thrasher, who reads everything I publish and always encourages me to write more.

I reserve my deepest thanks for my wife, Barbara Thrasher. If I have accomplished anything as a scholar, it is only because of her constant encouragement and support.

—Christopher Thrasher

This book is dedicated to my mother, Edith Lancaster, who helped keep me fed while this work was in progress, and who said she would be delighted to have a book dedicated to her, no matter how terrible the subject.

I have to thank Christopher Thrasher for undertaking this project with me. Christopher is an amazing historian with an attention to detail and dedication to nuance that have proven inspiring to me again and again.

My friend Michael Hodge got me started on this particular line of inquiry, and I'll always be thankful to him for that. Let me second Christopher's praise of the Garland County Historical Society, which is truly one of the best county historical societies in the state of Arkansas and one dedicated to bringing the full fruits of historical inquiry and preservation to the local community.

This manuscript has undergone multiple visions and revisions, and I must thank everyone who has provided feedback on any of the various versions. Too, the Arkansas State Archives and the Butler Center for Arkansas Studies at the Central Arkansas Library System have worked to make access to state newspapers easier through projects of digitization, which greatly facilitated the writing of this book.

And finally, I am perpetually indebted to my wife, Anna, whose sweet love remembered such wealth brings, that then I scorn to change my state with kings.

—Guy Lancaster

CHAPTER 1

INTRODUCTION

Up with the kettle
And down with the pan
And give us a penny
To bury the wren

—*Traditional Irish "Wren's Day" song*

Oscar Chitwood was lynched, to begin with. There was no doubt whatever about that.

At least, for a few days. But soon enough, the story of the mob—that, the world had been told, came and shot Oscar Chitwood to death on December 26, 1910, there at the county courthouse in Hot Springs, Arkansas—utterly fell apart. As much as locals wanted to believe Deputy John Rutherford's claims on this matter, all the evidence rather too convincingly argued the contrary, and so in 1911, Rutherford and another deputy, Ben Murray, were indicted for the premeditated murder of Chitwood.

Granted, Chitwood would have been a likely candidate for a lynching. He was a white man living in the South at a time by which the practice of lynching had largely hardened along racial lines, but white men were still occasionally executed by vigilante mobs in this time and place, especially when they were held responsible for the death of popular lawmen, like Sheriff Jake Houpt, whose image graces the cover of this book and who

Vicksburg Evening Post.

[...]UME XXVIII. VICKSBURG, MISSISSIPPI, MONDAY, DECEMBER 26, 1910. No. 309.

[...]ER 300 FREE XMAS DINNERS SENT OUT

[...]LVATION ARMY DOES A FINE [...]HARITABLE WORK AND [...]INGS JOY TO MANY SAD [...]EARTS—CAPT. BELCHER BUSY

[...]e Salvation Army people have [...] very busy for the last few days [...]ding out Christmas dinners and [...] relief work to bring joy and [...] to the poor of the city. 315 [...] have been provided this year. [...] Belcher states that he be- [...] that this has been one of the [...] successful Xmas celebrations [...] he has ever given to the poor [...] of this or any other city and [...] the people that were reached this [...] he knows to be quite worthy.

[...] was announced that the baskets [...] be distributed, beginning Sat- [...], Dec. 24th, at 2 p.m. and even

SHAKE UP IN TAFT'S CABINET

Washington, Dec. 26.—The Department's last weeks, was cited here today as a basis for the revival of rumors of a shake-up in Taft's cabinet early in the new year. The rumors include the resignation of Secretaries Knox, Ballinger, MacVeagh, and possibly Wilson. Credence is given the report that Congressman Charles Scott, of Kansas, chairman of the commiteet on agriculture, is a candidate to succeed Wilson. MacVeagh's resignation would be traced to ill-health, it is rumored. C. D. Norton, secretary to the President, may succeed him. Senator Flint, of California, and Representative Tawney, of Minnesota, are picked to succeed Ballinger.

LADY ACCIDENTALLY KILLED BY PISTOL.

Jackson, Miss., Dec. 26.—News from Tampa, Fla., says that the death of Mrs. I. O. Harrell, formerly Miss Collie Weathersby, of this city, which oc-

Oscar Chitwood, White Murderer, Lynched by Mob

Hot Springs, Ark., Dec. 26.—Oscar Chitwood, a white mountaineer, charged with murdering Sheriff Jake Houpt in Hot Springs last August, was intercepted by a mob early this morning, as deputies attempted to spirit him from the county jail, and shot dead. His body was riddled with bullets. Deputies attempted to remove Chitwood from jail to a prison, when warned that a mob of Houpt's friends were forming. Chitwood was taken from the rear door of the jail by Deputy John Rutherford. Two blocks from jail, and almost in the center of the city, thirty men overpowered the deputy and seized the prisoner. The mob was prepared to lynch Chitwood, and the sight of him prompted speedier means. A hundred shots were fired.

Chitwood was awaiting trial for murder. He was recently granted a change of venue, and would have been taken to Benton, Ark., for trial today.

Houpt was killed in a street fight when Oscar and George Chitwood, brothers, began shooting up the town. George then wounded, died. Oscar narrowly escaped lynching then, and was placed in the penitentiary for safe-keeping.

Houpt's friends resented the change of venue and determined to storm the jail and prevent his removal to Benton. None of the lynchers were recognized, as they wore handkerchief masks.

The police immediately started an investigation, claiming they had information that may identify at least one of the lynchers. Chitwood's body was taken to the morgue, and an inquest will probably be held this afternoon.

GUNBOAT SENT TO HONDURAS

Washington, Dec. 26.—Following reports of serious trouble in Honduras, Secretary of the Navy Meyer today ordered the gunboat Yorktown to proceed immediately from Corinton, Nicaragua, to Amapala, Honduras. The official order to the commander said: "Observe and report upon the conditions existing on the western coast of Honduras." Amapala is believed to be the center of Bonilla's activities.

228 CITIES—28,508,007 PEOPLE.

Director Durand Makes Analysis Of Census Report.

Washington, Dec. 26.—Of the 92,000,000 people in the United States, more than twenty-eight and a half millions reside in cities exceeding 25,000,000 in population as shown by a recapitulation by the census bureau.

There are 228 of these cities. Nineteen of them have a population exceeding 100,000. The exact population of thetwo hundred and twenty-

SHERIFF HARDING DISPOSES OF THE BRIBE MONEY

DIVIDES IT AMONG FOUR WORTHY ORGANIZATIONS—SENATOR BILBO'S PERTINENT LETTER IN REGARD TO MONEY.

Jackson, Miss., Dec. 24, 1910.

To the People of Mississippi:

By virute of my position as the Sheriff of Hinds County, Foreman J. C. Cavett of the Grand Jury, turned over to me the alleged bribe money, which had been turned over to the Grand Jury by Hon. T. G. Bilbo, amounting to $645.00.

The trial having ended and the money being in my possession and without claimant therefor, and having received the following letter from Hon. T. G. Bilbo:

"Poplarville, Miss., Dec. 22, 1910.

"Col. R. J. Harding, Sheriff of Hinds

Front page of the December 26, 1910 *Vicksburg Evening Post*.

had, earlier in 1910, been killed in a shootout with Oscar Chitwood and his brother, George. But the young outlaw did not die at the hands of any mob. There is little doubt whatever about that.

This fact did not stop Oscar Chitwood's name from appearing on many nationally circulating lists of lynching victims. Typically, organizations that assembled such lists, like the National Association for the Advancement of Colored People (NAACP) and the Tuskegee Institute, based their work on nationally circulating newspapers. The initial story of the "lynching" of Chitwood did spread nationally, but those same newspapers did not follow the subsequent developments, the doubts and, later, the indictments, and scholars basing their work on these inventories have unwittingly included the Chitwood murder as an example of white-on-white lynching even well into the twenty-first century.

But what, though, was the real difference? Policemen had rather coyly been involved in lynchings previously, be it by informing mob leaders when a prisoner was expected to be transferred or by turning over the keys to the local jail after members of the mob made the necessary pretense of surprising the lawman on his rounds and holding him at gunpoint. After the fact, many of these policemen claimed to recognize no one from the mob, even if the lynching happened in the full light of day and the mob went about its task unmasked. The historical record is replete with lynchings that were facilitated by, at a bare minimum, the inactivity of sworn officers of the law at crucial points in time.

However, policemen coldly perpetrating a 2:00 a.m. assassination—and making such a hash of things that even those who would have been glad to be rid of Chitwood could not fail to notice certain discrepancies—seemed a bridge too far for many. The official push toward something like justice was probably aided by the less-than-stellar reputation of local law enforcement, the late Sheriff Houpt excepted, due to a whole history of corruption and double dealing that made Hot Springs a byword even in a state like Arkansas. One can easily imagine that, had Deputies Rutherford and Murray but covered their tracks just a little better, the history books would record Chitwood's killing even today as one more tragic enumeration of a form of violence so decidedly American. But this was not meant to be.

And there are lessons for us in that.

As reported in the September 26, 1922 edition of the *Sentinel-Record* newspaper in Hot Springs, Judge Scott Wood of the local circuit court, while overseeing a grand jury investigation of alleged vigilantes, issued the following defense of the tradition of law and order over and above the sort of "justice" meted out by "men in secret conclave," such as the Ku Klux Klan: "If the courts and juries should approve or palliate the use of unlawful means to promote the public good, public good would soon be merely the pretext for the use of all kinds of unlawful means to carry out the arbitrary will of an organization, which would usurp the powers of government and substitute its dictum, its night riders, its tar and feathers and its whip for the dignified and orderly processes of the courts of this country." The judge also cited a contemporary incident in Shreveport, Louisiana, in which "a number of negroes working in the railroad shops" received notices "purporting to be from the Ku Klux Klan, that they must quit work, that the Klan only warned once and if their warnings was not obeyed their punishment would be inflicted on the offender." Although, as Wood notes, the Klan denied responsibility for the affair, this incident demonstrated "that the organization cannot exist without having designing persons use the terror which it inspires to satisfy their own petty grudges and desires."

Several modern instances of well-publicized violence, killings by both police and vigilantes, have been connected rhetorically to the history of American lynching. So, it behooves us to develop a deeper appreciation of the fluidity of such a category, to understand that a general toleration for the practice of lynching opened up a path for all manner of exploitation under the guise of "the will of the people" or "popular sovereignty." The murder of Oscar Chitwood was precisely the sort of event that could happen in a society that tolerated lynching.

This book begins with a short survey of the history of Hot Springs up to the point right before the murder of Chitwood, not only because it is important to establish a sense of place for any story we might tell but also because that larger history plays a role in why certain members of the local constabulary imagined that they could get away with murdering one of their prisoners—and why the town rather quickly turned on them and demanded justice. Hot Springs, after all, was a nationally known "spa city" attracting elite visitors from across the United States, a center of culture nestled in a state often regarded as its antithesis. And Hot Springs also had a reputation as one of the wildest cities in the state, a den of debauchery nestled within a bastion of conservatism.

After that, we survey the history of the Chitwood affair up to the point of his murder, and then we will demonstrate that Chitwood, although not lynched himself, was exactly the sort of man who would have been targeted by a secret mob, and so the initial story that circulated in the newspapers was fundamentally believable. Up to a point. But that initial assumption proved unprovable, and so next, we follow the doubts that arose and the subsequent indictment and trial of the police officers involved in what, it became clear, was actually an assassination. And then, with our conclusion, we explore how the story of the Chitwood affair demands that we revise some of our assumptions about the nature of vigilantism in America.

Arkansas Gazette.

NINETY-SECOND YEAR. LITTLE ROCK, TUESDAY, JANUARY, 3, 1911. PRIC

DEPUTIES HELD RESPONSIBLE IN CHITWOOD CASE

Coroner's Jury Returns Verdict Against John Rutherford and Ben Murray and Recommends They Be Held

AGAINST "OTHERS UNKNOWN"

Both Are Now in Jail, Being Held Without Bail, and Will Remain Until Court Convenes.

ASKS SPECIAL GRAND JURY

OHIO VOTE BUYING CASE BRINGS THRONG TO TOWN

West Union Hotels and Rooming Houses Crowded With Offenders—Total Reaches 1,431.

West Union, O., Jan. 2.—Judge A. Z. Blair held court late tonight in order to receive confessions of those corrupted in election bribery. By 6 o'clock over 300 persons indicted had been arraigned. As the town was filled with offenders anxious to get in their pleas, it was decided to continue the court session as late as possible.

All hotel, boarding and rooming houses space was taxed and many private homes were turned open to visitors.

Although Prosecutor Shivley and Sheriff J. P. Williams, both newly elected, assumed office today, there was no cessation in the remarkable activity displayed in the bribery cases. The Grand Jury tonight reported 183 new indictments a new record for one day, which brings the total indicted to 1,431.

Judge Blair was called upon today to disfranchise a boyhood playmate, the son of a man who had befriended him in his youth.

SIX DIE IN TRAIN CRASH

Collision Near Rainsville, Ky., Brings Death and Injury.

Ashland, Ky., Jan. 2.—Six persons

HIGHER EFFICIENCY NEED OF RAILWAYS

Louis Y. Brandies Denies Necessity for Increased Rates in Brief Filed With Interstate Commerce Commission.

CONSUMER SHOULD BE WARY

Urges Public to Rebel at Ever-Increasing Rates and Ever-[illegible] Cost of Liv[illegible]

Washington, Jan. 2.—[illegible] standards of efficiency, not [illegible] freight charges, are the [illegible] needs today of American railways [illegible] proposition is the essence of th[illegible] filed today with the Interstate [illegible] Commission by Louis D. [illegible] of Boston, counsel for the T[illegible] Committee of Commercial organi[illegible] of the Atlantic Seaboard in the [illegible] by the commission of the proposed advances in freight rates by carriers in official classification territory—that part of the country east of the Mississippi and

TENNESSEE REGULARS CAPTURE THE SENATE

Fusionists, However, Gain Control of House Organization—Balloting for Senatorship Next Week.

Nashville, Tenn., Jan. 2.—The regular Democrats captured the machinery of the Senate and the fusionists the house organization at the opening of the 57th biennial session of the Tennessee General Assembly here today. In the Senate the regular slate, including the election of N. Baxter, Jr., as speaker, went through easily. In the house A. M. Leach was chosen with less than a quorum of representatives present. On the final vote on permanent organization the regulars refrained from voting. The fusion forces expect enough regulars will come over tomorrow to make a quorum but this is considered extremely unlikely.

Half a dozen or more notices of contest were filed by fusionists in the house this afternoon and at least two senatorial seats will be contested. One of these latter is by a Republican and the other by a regular. As the fusionists appear to seat the contestants and will probably do so unless the regulars join in the proceedings.

The first balloting for United States senator may take place next Tuesday week. The date hinges entirely upon the question whether or not the legislature will be held to be permanently organized by tomorrow.

WHITNEY SUPPORTS LODGE

WEATHER PLAYS CURIOUS PRANKS

Montreal, Canada, Enjoys Temperature of 32, While in Little Rock Thermometer Sinks to 13.

WILL BE COLDER TODAY

Cold Weather Causes Suffering and Charitable Organizations Are Besieged by the Poverty-Stricken.

Old Boreas seemed to have been showing off his ability to play queer pranks when he came roaring down through the Southwest yesterday morning, bursting water pipes and almost knocking the bottom out of the thermometer, while Detroit, Mich., was enjoying balmy spring-like weather at 46 degrees above and up in Montreal, Can., the mercury had dropped only to the freezing point of 32 degrees above.

The minimum temperature reached in Little Rock during the day yesterday was 13 above, and at no time in the day did it go higher than 20. As the

ARKANSAS WEATHER FORECAST.
Fair and continued cold, Tuesday and Wednesday.

LOCAL RECORD YESTERDAY.

	Bar.	Tem.	Wind.	Wth.	Prec.
7 a. m.	30.34	14	NW	Clear	0.00
7 p. m.	30.47	20	N	Cloudy	0.00

Maximum temperature 20, minimum 12 degrees.

ENJOYS LAST FEW HOURS OF LIBERTY

Convicted Murderer Must Enter Penitentiary Thursday, but Proposes to Have a Good Time Until Then.

Somewhere in the confines of the city, J. P. Henslee of Clark county, under sentence of 10 years in the state penitentiary for murder in the second degree, is making the most of the short time that stretches between him and the grim, gray prison walls.

On the 20th of April, 1910, following a slight altercation, Henslee shot and killed a neighbor, Walter Legate. He was tried and convicted in the Clark County Circuit Court of murder in the second degree, and sentenced to 10 years in the penitentiary. Appeal was taken to the Supreme Court, but the decision of the lower court was sustained, the opinion being handed [illegible]

Front page of the January 3, 1911 *Arkansas Gazette.*

Policeman John Rutherford was eventually exonerated by a jury of his apparent peers, and Ben Murray never stood trial. They forever insisted that a mob had gunned down their prisoner during his transfer to another facility. They insisted that Chitwood was lynched. But even from this far remove, the evidence against these two men is overwhelming.

Oscar Chitwood was not lynched. There is no doubt whatever about that.

CHAPTER 2

A VERY BRIEF HISTORY OF HOT SPRINGS, ARKANSAS

However, it will not be very long before every person will wear a genial and contented smile upon their face on account of having the satisfaction to know that Hot Springs is the liveliest and gayest town in the United States.

—Arkansas Democrat, *November 4, 1878*

Hot Springs is a complicated place, and no short survey of its past can ever do it justice. One of the oldest American settlements in Arkansas, it has also lost a lot of its history through fire, flood and neglect. The apparent epitome of civilization, with a downtown area regularly compared to the spa cities of Europe, the city also has a history marked by lawlessness and corruption more akin to some outpost of the Wild West. Renowned as a den of sin rife with gambling, prostitution and booze, Hot Springs has also been a force in reactionary conservative politics and has, at times, warred against those industries that sustained its economy.

One of the most enduring legends surrounding Hot Springs holds that Native Americans of various tribes came to the site to partake of the thermal waters, and all tribes declared the site a "valley of peace" and abided amicably among each other during their stay.[1] These legends must have begun early on, for Hiram Abiff Whittington, who settled in Hot Springs in the 1830s, wrote in an 1833 letter to his brother that the site of the springs "was always considered sacred ground. Hostile tribes on meeting here, (no matter how inveterate they were towards each other) embraced as brothers,

Hot Springs in 1875. *Courtesy of Hot Springs National Park.*

the tomahawk was buried, and the pipe (emblem of peace and love) was passed from a member of one hostile tribe to that of another. I wish I could say the same of the whites since they have settled here."[2] And throughout the history of Hot Springs, the railroad companies, bathhouses, hotels and other tourist attractions all promoted their own variations on this myth, so much so that now these legends remain difficult to dislodge. In 2007, Mark Blaeuer of the National Park Service published perhaps the best synthesis of the evidence proving an American Indian presence in and around Hot Springs, a short book titled *Didn't All the Indians Come Here? Separating Fact from Fiction at Hot Springs National Park*. As Blaeuer stated from the outset: "My own short answer to the book's title question would be 'No.'"[3]

In the vicinity of the city are a number of sites where Natives mined novaculite, a sedimentary rock easily used for chipped stone tools, during the Archaic period, a period spanning roughly 9500 to 650 BC. The Jones Mill Site in neighboring Hot Spring County, for example, shows signs of habitation for nearly 8,000 years, roughly from 6000 BC to AD 1450.[4] These would have been the ancestors of the Caddo Indians, a cultural group that, at the time of the expedition of Spanish conquistador Hernando de Soto, was present in southwestern Arkansas. However, as Blaeuer notes, "No unambiguously bathing-related prehistoric artifacts have ever been found" around the site of the springs.[5] Moreover, the fact that downtown Hot Springs

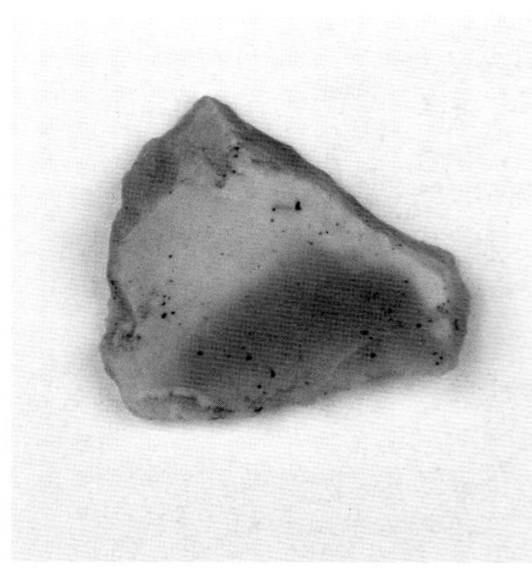

Novaculite scraper from Hot Springs. *Courtesy of Hot Springs National Park.*

has undergone more than two centuries of landscaping, often using fill from the Ouachita River bottomlands miles away, "may have rendered soil around the springs unreliable for an archeological test relating to area prehistory."[6]

There are diverse accounts of various Natives, either singly or in small groups, traveling through the area in the early nineteenth century and even making use of the springs.[7] But the legends of an American Indian presence in the area stem not from such documented history but from various pamphlets and books published by the railroad industry. For example, James William (J.W.) Buel, a prolific producer of sensational "true stories," published in 1880 (likely at the behest of the Iron Mountain Railroad) the book *Legends of the Ozarks*, which contained a number of Indian legends about Hot Springs.[8] Other such books and pamphlets include *The Hot Springs of Arkansas: America's Baden-Baden Illustrated: Where It Is, And How to Get There* (1880), *Cutter's Guide to the Hot Springs of Arkansas* (1882) and *Ye Hot Springs, Ark., Picture Booke* (1893). Such confabulation was not unique to Hot Springs alone; as historian Thomas A. Chambers has written, "Proprietors of springs resorts invented, adopted, and promoted their own histories in hopes of attracting travelers who shared these ideals of a romanticized past."[9] And the manufacture of these legends may have been a product of the time, too. According to Blaeuer, "The idea of a peaceful valley might have had even more appeal in the late nineteenth century, when America was trying, at least ostensibly, to unify itself, thus healing wounds suffered in and just after the Civil War. Health-seekers came from both North and South to comparatively cosmopolitan Hot Springs, Arkansas."[10]

Just as legends tie various Natives to Hot Springs, so, too, do they make Hernando de Soto an early visitor. Such legends did not emerge organically but were, in part, manufactured for purposes of developing tourism; as early as 1893, the Missouri Pacific Railroad published *The Discovery of Hot Springs, Ark. By DeSoto*.[11] The U.S. Congress established the United States De Soto Expedition Commission on August 26, 1935, for purposes of establishing the path by which Hernando de Soto and his troops traveled through the American Southeast. John W. Swanton, a Smithsonian Institute anthropologist, headed the commission, the vice chair of which was John R. Fordyce, an engineer and business leader of Hot Springs who was also an amateur archaeologist (and the son of Samuel Fordyce, mentioned later in this chapter). According to Blaeuer, John R. Fordyce recreated part of the de Soto route working from a piece (perhaps translated by his wife, Lillian) in a French-language book, the name of which remains unknown. From what Blaeuer can reconstruct, the book may have purported to be a translation of Garcilaso de la Vega's account of the expedition (originally published in 1605) but was actually "unmistakably fiction" and "laden with verbal ornaments" of "the late nineteenth century and the early twentieth century, when such counterfeits were common."[12] To support his version of de Soto's journey, in 1930, Fordyce began displaying a halberd he claimed was used by the expedition. After many years of controversy, the Arkansas Archeological Survey concluded in 2014 that the halberd was probably from the de Soto expedition, although it was recovered from the White River and not anywhere near Hot Springs.[13] Later reconstructions of de Soto's route, most notably by anthropologist Charles Hudson, corrected Fordyce's advocacy for his hometown and relocated the route away from Hot Springs.[14] Despite the overwhelming scholarly acceptance of Hudson's route for the de Soto expedition, however, the Swanton report, published in 1939, had decades of circulation before it was challenged and continues to be a touchstone for local history.[15]

In 1804, President Thomas Jefferson commissioned not only the Lewis and Clark expedition to explore the land of the Louisiana Purchase but also two other men, William Dunbar and Dr. George Hunter, both of them scientists, to lead an expedition up the Red, Black and Ouachita Rivers. One of the sites they intended to explore and study was the hot springs of Arkansas, about which they had already heard a number of accounts of bubbling fountains of healing waters. On December 7, 1804, the expedition had reached the Ouachita River's closest point to the hot springs, and the following day, they set off on foot for the site, where they would spend the next four weeks engaged in study, not only of the area's geology but also of the local flora and fauna. The expedition encountered no Natives here; the only sign of habitation was a handful of shacks and one log cabin some distance from the springs, likely used by transient hunters and trappers. Of particular interest to the men was the source of the water's constant temperature, and though they never determined it, Dunbar did discover microorganisms capable of living in the hot water, which, as historian Trey Berry notes, "may be one of the first North American reports of such

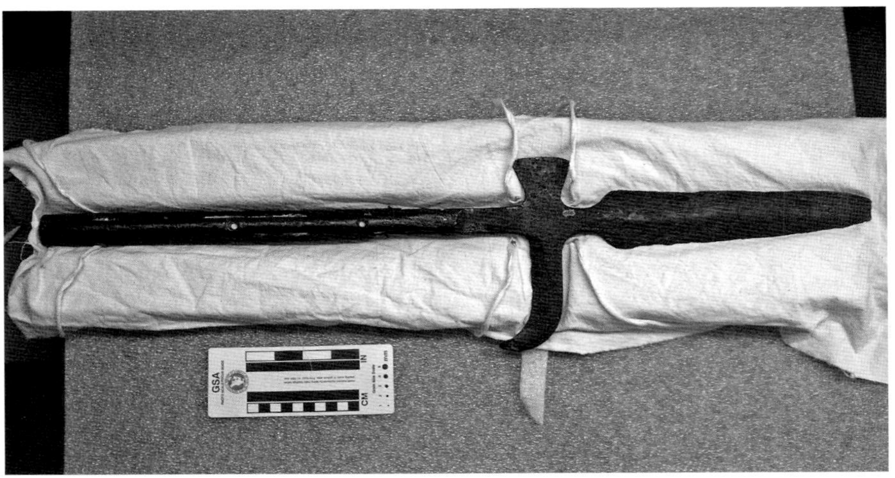

Halberd head, probably used by the de Soto expedition. *Courtesy of Hot Springs National Park.*

Early cabin in Hot Springs. *Courtesy of Hot Springs National Park.*

creatures (thermophiles/extremophiles) existing in such hostile aquatic environments."[16] Major Stephen Harriman Long was the next explorer to visit the area, passing through on January 1, 1818, on a return from the Red River. He took note of about fifteen cabins, all unoccupied at that time of year. Two of the twenty-two springs were equipped with sweathouses, four with rude tubes and one with both.[17] He published his observations later that year in an article titled "Hot Springs of the Washitaw" in the *American Monthly Magazine and Critical Reviews*.

Sources differ as to the identity of the first permanent white settler in what is now Hot Springs. Some accounts have Louisiana planter Emmanuel Prudhomme establishing a home there in 1807, but he may have been only an occasional visitor. The first permanent settler may, in fact, have been John Perciful, who settled there in 1809; he repaired the temporary cabins hammered together by some visitors and took on the role of concierge, providing summer residents the staples they needed to make their stay a relatively comfortable one. By 1820, his wife was running a boardinghouse. Five years later, the family of Josiah Millard (also spelled Mellard) arrived in the area and assembled a dogtrot-style cabin considered by some to be the first hotel in Hot Springs. By the early 1830s, the springs were proving a major attraction, attracting renowned travelers such as Thomas Nuttall, Henry Rowe Schoolcraft and George Featherstonhaugh.[18] In 1832, Congress passed legislation proposed by Arkansas's territorial delegate, Ambrose H. Sevier, to set aside the area called the Hot Springs Reservation (now known as Hot Springs National Park) for federal use, exempting it from settlement. Later that decade, regular stagecoach service between Little Rock and Hot Springs was established, making it possible for numerous "invalids" to visit the area. By 1851, Hot Springs was home to two rows of hotels, along with the bathhouses and the usual concomitant businesses, and the city attracted not only numerous invalids hoping to find relief from their condition in the area's thermal waters but also many seekers of leisure.[19]

However, the ownership of the land containing the actual springs remained contested for many decades. Among the earliest claimants was Don Juan Filhiol, a Frenchman who served with Spanish troops against the English in Spanish West Florida during the American Revolutionary War; he later established the Arkansas settlement of Ecore a Fabri (now the city of Camden) along the Ouachita River. According to family history, for his service, he was given a Spanish land grant for the area now encompassing the hot springs and reportedly sold it in 1803 but repurchased it in 1806. Filhiol died intestate in 1821, and efforts by his younger son, Gammont, to have the legality of his father's claim recognized continued on through 1830 but were ultimately unsuccessful.[20]

In 1828, Ludovicus and Lydia Bassett Belding settled in what is now Hot Springs, having moved from Massachusetts and likely choosing Hot Springs as Lydia's parents had already settled there. By the following year, Ludovicus had begun the first in a series of business ventures. For example, he leased a boardinghouse from one John Perciful and refurbished it. He soon subleased the boardinghouse to others and bought a farm, called Gulpha Landing, south of the town. Ludovicus laid claim to a part of the land around the hot springs site, based on the Preemption Act of 1830, and when he died in 1833, his wife continued to pursue the claim.[21]

Another claimant was Henry Massie Rector, who would later, as governor, take Arkansas into the Confederate side of the Civil War in 1861. Rector's father, Elias Rector, had acquired a claim to the hot springs through the purchase of a New Madrid Certificate issued to François Langlois. Langlois's original land claim encompassed two hundred arpents in southeastern Missouri that had been affected by the New Madrid earthquakes of 1811–12, which rendered a great deal of land in Missouri, Arkansas and Tennessee uninhabitable. Thus had Langlois, according to historian Regina A. Bates, "by the New Madrid Act of February 17, 1815, been allowed to locate a like quantity of land on any of the United States lands of Missouri Territory then authorized to be sold."[22] (What is now Arkansas was part of Missouri Territory until 1819.) Elias Rector tried to use the New Madrid Certificate to claim the land around the hot springs but ran into trouble, as the land had not yet been surveyed. He willed the claim to his son, Henry Massie Rector, but by the time Henry arrived in Arkansas Territory in 1835 to look after his father's land claims, the time by which Congress had allowed such titles to be completed had already passed. Too, Congress had, three years previously, created the Hot Springs Reservation, which voided any private appropriation of the hot springs. However, Rector continued to press his claim through the years.[23]

The Belding and Rector families were not the only ones with ostensible claims to the Hot Springs. Sarah Perciful tried to file a claim to the same land in 1835, asserting that she and her late husband, John, had occupied and improved the land in accordance with the Preemption Act of 1814. However, she was denied both times she filed her claim. In 1841, John "Cyrus" Hale, who had recently moved to the area, bought half of her claim, purchasing the rest after Sarah's death in 1849. In a bid to strengthen their hands, Hale and Rector purchased a share in each other's claims.[24] Meanwhile, the Belding heirs, led by Major William H. Gaines (Lydia Belding's son-in-law) were, in 1851, denied permission to enter the lands they claimed by Alexander Stuart, the secretary of the interior, based on the fact that the land constituted a federal reserve. Stuart later reversed his decision, allowing the family to enter. The fact that Attorney General Caleb Cushing issued an 1854 opinion nullifying all claims—again, with reference to the 1832 act creating the reservation—did not hinder ongoing litigation.[25] A lower court had permitted the Gaines family to evict Hale, who subsequently appealed the case all the way to the United States Supreme Court. The 1860 ruling of *Hale v. Gaines* upheld the decision.[26]

In 1869, the three main litigants appealed to Congress, and in 1874, the Court of Claims ruled for the federal government. The United States Supreme Court upheld the decision on appeal.[27] Congress redefined the Hot Springs Reservation in 1877, establishing the Hot Springs Commission, which redrew reservation boundaries and sold lots for land that now fell outside its more limited boundaries. For the first time, the government also began stationing federal officials at Hot Springs and began leasing spots for the construction of bathhouses along what is now Bathhouse Row. But the final settlement of claims on the land did not immediately simplify local operations. As historian Sharon Shugart observes: "Not all of the improvements had been made by the claimants themselves. Unable to develop the entire town at once, Rector, the Hales, and Gainses and the Beldings had sublet property to hundreds of people who had built homes, business, churches, and schools upon it."[28] The drawn-out legal disputes and their aftermath meant that much of the town was a ramshackle mess—after all, few people wanted to invest in permanent structures if the latest legal wrinkle could deprive them of their rights to land and businesses. As Shugart writes, "It is impossible to know how long this state of affairs might have lasted had not a devastating fire in 1878 burned most of the area on the central and south end of the town to the ground."[29] That fire, combined with the end of the legal battle, paved the way for the sturdier, more modern construction that would define the town in its golden age.

The Ouachita Mountains region in which Hot Springs is located did not attract the large-scale capitalist development common to eastern and southern Arkansas in the antebellum era, the sort of development predicated on the use of slave labor. The region's rugged land precluded the profitable production of crops like cotton, and its rivers were not the most easily navigable—indeed, antebellum steamboats could typically traverse the

Ouachita River only as far as Camden or Arkadelphia to the south. The land thus remained poorly populated when compared to other parts of the state, and the slave population was proportionally lower, too. By 1860, the number of slaves in Hot Spring County—the location of the city of Hot Springs prior to the creation of Garland County in 1873—was 613, just over 10 percent of the total population of 5,635. Many worked at the hotels of Hot Springs, and one hotel even advertised that its warm baths were available for "invalid Negroes," who would then be shipped back to their homes after treatment.[30] The aforementioned Belding family, among the original claimants for the land surrounding the hot springs, owned slaves, with Lydia recording 7 in her possession according to the 1850 Slave Schedules. The family also staunchly supported the Confederacy, with her son Albert being captured by Union forces in Missouri in 1864.[31] However, just as they did all across the country, once the enslaved in Arkansas became free, they embraced education with enthusiasm. There are records of two schools operated by the Freedmen's Bureau operating in the Hot Springs area in the late 1860s, as well as a school established by Roanoke Baptist Church, a Black congregation that built its house of worship in the Whittington Avenue area in 1868.[32]

During the Civil War, some local residents in and around Hot Springs did support the Confederacy, with men flocking to both Hot Springs and Rockport (which was then the county seat) to enlist, and many of these eventually became part of the Third Arkansas Cavalry. In addition, local citizens made material and financial contributions to the war effort, with Hiram Abiff Whittington pledging one hundred dollars.[33] In 1862, Governor Henry Massie Rector briefly relocated the state government to Hot Springs amid fears of a Federal advance on Little Rock, but Hot Springs served as the "capital" only from May 6 to July 14, 1862.[34]

However, there was a significant Unionist sentiment among these hillfolk, and Union recruitment drives in the Ouachita Mountains regularly met with success.[35] As historian Tom DeBlack has written, "Northern and western Arkansas would continue to be Unionist strongholds throughout the course of the war. Despite having the third-smallest white population, Arkansas would provide more troops for the Federal army than any other Confederate state except Tennessee."[36] One noteworthy band of Unionist sympathizers and Confederate deserters operating in the Ouachita Mountains was led by an Arkadelphia man named Andy Brown. On February 15, 1863, a Confederate Homeguard unit tracked these men to McGraw's (or McGrew's) Mill, on the Walnut Fork of the Ouachita River about halfway between Hot Springs and Mount Ida. After heavy skirmishing

A rebel guerrilla raid in a western town. *Courtesy of Library of Congress.*

that resulted in the deaths of eleven members of the Unionist band and one Confederate, Brown's men retreated, and twenty-seven of their number made their way to Union-controlled Fayetteville in northwestern Arkansas three weeks later.[37] During a November 1863 expedition from Benton to Mount Ida, Lieutenant Henry C. Caldwell of the Third Iowa Cavalry and his men stayed briefly in Hot Springs before proceeding on to Caddo Gap in Montgomery County and then hurrying on toward Mount Ida. Along the way, his forces recruited "nearly 300 loyal men, who had come from the surrounding mountains to join the Federal Army." Many of these men were "compelled to flee their homes to save themselves from being hanged by the rebels," and Caldwell recorded several stories of guerrillas "robbing, persecuting, imprisoning, and hanging Union men."[38]

After the Civil War, Hot Springs grew at a far more rapid clip than did the rest of the state. As historian Wendy Richter has noted, while the state population grew by only 11 percent between 1860 and 1870, Hot Springs grew from 201 to 1,276, an increase of more than six times over. Men of military age comprised a significant portion of this growth, suggesting to Richter "that their exposure to the area during the Civil War played an important role in the growth that took place."[39] The Black population also grew during this period. As before the war, the service industry was a major employer of African Americans. Joe Golden, a former slave who worked in Hot Springs, observed in an interview with the Works Progress Administration, "Hot Springs was a good place to make money. Lots of rich folks was coming to the hotels."[40] With the establishment of a public school district in Hot Springs in 1881, African American children were educated at the Rugg School; later renamed the Langston School, it did not serve all twelve grades until the twentieth century, graduating its first high school class only in 1910.[41]

Not only did African Americans have access to employment in Hot Springs, but they also had access to the same sorts of facilities that attracted wealthy whites to the area. According to park interpreter Gail Payton Sears, Black patrons in the 1880s could pay to bathe at the Ozark Bathhouse, the Independent Bathhouse and possibly the Rammelsberg Bathhouse on Bathhouse Row, though not during the period from ten o'clock in the morning to noon, the optimum time for bathing prescribed by physicians.[42] This segregation, says James Byrd, was "apparently enforced through social custom rather than federal, state, or city regulation." In response to this segregation, many local African Americans applied for permission from the federal government to construct bathhouses for use by Black residents and visitors but made little headway, their applications being "denied without explanation while white applicants would have their projects accepted."[43] The first bathhouse intended for the exclusive use of a Black clientele, the Crystal Bathhouse, opened in 1904 on the edge of the Black business district. Though it burned in 1913, there opened the following year at the same site the Pythian Hotel Bathhouse, another Black business. African Americans also worked as porters and attendants at all the major bathhouses save the Buckstaff, which advertised itself as having only white attendants.[44] African Americans could even achieve some measure of political success in Hot Springs, as exemplified by the career of Jackson D. Page. After working as a census enumerator, policeman and barber, he was elected to the position of justice of the peace, serving during 1883–84. In 1886, he and J.H. Golden, also Black, were elected as aldermen in Hot Springs. Page was also the first African American admitted to the bar in Garland County and reportedly counted leading white citizens among his clientele. His credentials were accepted by the Supreme Court of Arkansas in 1908.[45]

The general attraction of Hot Springs for relatively wealthy people seeking medical cures or simply rest and relaxation, combined with the difficulty of getting to the place in the nineteenth century, made the routes into the city an attractive target for bandits. As historian Orval E. Allbritton

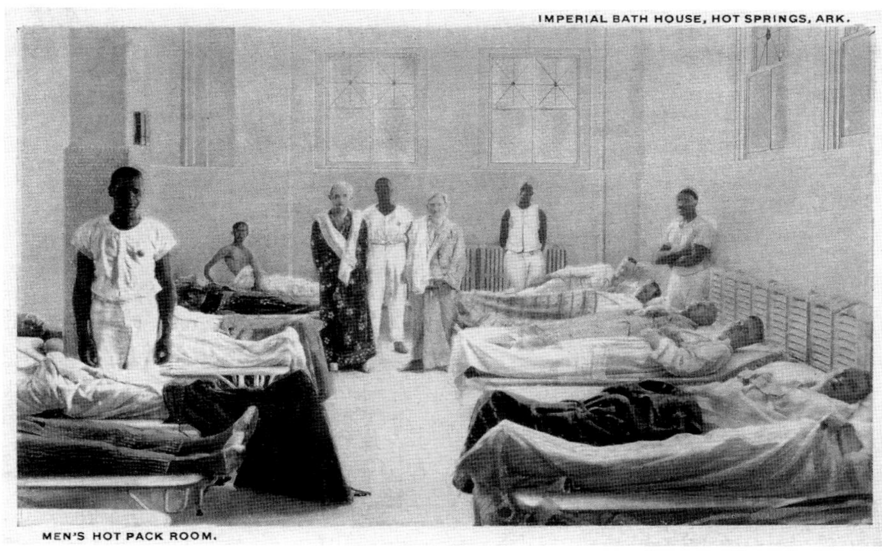

Unidentified bathhouse attendants with bathers in the Imperial Bathhouse. *Courtesy of Hot Springs National Park.*

African American tourists in Hot Springs. *Courtesy of Butler Center for Arkansas Studies, Central Arkansas Library System.*

writes, "Most visitors journeyed by the Iron Mountain Railroad" from Little Rock "to Malvern, twenty-five miles east of Hot Springs, and then boarded the El Paso Stage Line for the remainder of the trip. Although this was a short distance, it was a rough passage, the road dusty in the summer and extremely muddy in the rainy season."[46] These were ideal conditions for bandits on horseback, and perhaps none who targeted this line were more famous than the James and Younger Gang. According to Allbritton, at least three of the gang members—Jesse James, Frank James and Cole Younger—had visited Hot Springs before. On the morning of January 15, 1874, five blue-coated men on horseback intercepted the El Paso stage on the last leg of its journey to Hot Springs, on the west bank of Gulpha Creek just outside of town. The riders ordered the stage to halt and its passengers to exit, whereupon they were robbed of their valuables; two other wagons came upon the scene, and they, too, were stopped and rifled. Among the passengers was John Albyne Burbank, the former governor of Dakota Territory, who personally lost $840 in cash, along with a diamond pin and gold watch. After being relieved of his valuables, Burbank asked for the return of his personal papers, and there was a tense moment when one of the robbers, spreading the papers over the ground to examine them, said, "Boys, I believe he is a detective—shoot him." However, the leader of the gang waved away the pointing guns of his comrades and returned the former governor's papers to him.[47] Years later, with their life of crime behind them, the last two surviving members of the James and Younger gang made their own separate visits to Hot Springs. Cole Younger appeared on stage at the Hot Springs City Auditorium in 1909 as part of a lecture circuit and, in passing, remarked about the changes the city had undergone since the 1870s. Frank James returned to Hot Springs in either 1911 or 1912 and worked briefly at Happy Hollow, a small amusement park, greeting people and selling souvenirs.[48]

In 1876, the City of Hot Springs officially incorporated, allowing for the creation of a local government. As Allbritton observes, the decision was apparently in response to the increasing presence of "undesirables," with the incorporation petition including the line:

> *Your petitioners would state and show your honor that our community, or town is now being flooded with lewd and immoral characters who infest our streets day and night and by their obscene carriage and vulgar language render it absolutely disagreeable for persons of respectability to be on the streets and more especially on the Holy Sabbath, on account of which*

The Grande Promenade and the Arlington Hotel. *Courtesy of Library of Congress.*

> *many on that day are denied the privileges of attending the services of various churches, and that your petitioners believe that this state of facts will prove very detrimental, if not to our morals in fact at home to our moral reputation abroad.*[49]

But as will be seen, Hot Springs would prove sufficiently damaging to its own moral reputation abroad in a number of creative ways.

In 1875, perhaps the most famous hotel in Hot Springs history, the Arlington, first opened its doors on the site of today's Arlington Lawn. At the time, it was the largest hotel in Arkansas, featuring 120 rooms, and during the following decade, an annex of another 100 rooms was added.[50] As Hot Springs grew and attracted more and more visitors of the educated middle class, the first incarnation of the Arlington Hotel found itself no longer at the peak of luxury, especially after the 1890 construction of the 500-room Eastman Hotel. The stockholders of the Arlington Hotel Company thus decided to raze the current structure and rebuild along an even grander design, and in 1893, the second Arlington Hotel was opened to the public.

As local historian Ann Greene has observed, the Arlington benefited from "increasingly clever advertisements stressing the health and beauty benefits of the Spa" that "appeared in newspapers and magazines around the country," and the famous individuals who were drawn toward the Arlington included the likes of William Jennings Bryan, Bat Masterson, Jane Addams, General John J. Pershing, Philip Armour, Jack Dempsey, Andrew Carnegie, F.W. Woolworth, Evelyn Nesbit, John Barrymore and Lillian Russell.[51] The hotel managed to survive the fires of 1905 and 1913 but caught fire and burned in 1923. The third and final Arlington Hotel, which remains one of the most notable sites on the physical landscape of downtown Hot Springs, was completed in 1924 across the street from where the first and second incarnations stood.

A fire on March 5, 1878, destroyed a significant portion of the downtown area and left more than one thousand people homeless. As the *Arkansas Gazette* reported, the fire "broke out about 2 o'clock this morning in a negro shanty in the rear of the French Restaurant, in the heart of the city." From there, it spread rapidly in all directions for about half a mile, destroying some 150 buildings in the process. Although a number of hotels were destroyed, including the Hot Springs Hotel and the American Hotel, no one died, and neither was anyone injured, with the business district being largely abandoned at that hour of the night. Among the casualties were a number of dry goods stores, the post office, some jewelry stores, Central Bath House, the Knights of Pythias Hall and the offices of the *Sentinel* newspaper. The *Gazette* speculated that the fire, which raged for eight hours before being brought under control, might, "relatively speaking," be "the greatest disaster that has ever occurred to any town or city in America, the proportion of loss and homeless sufferers being greater than that occasioned by the great Chicago fire."[52]

Despite the destructive force of the fire, it actually made Hot Springs the nationally known resort it became. As Shugart writes, "Before the great fire of 1878 destroyed the south end of the business district, the reservation and the city were marred with ramshackle buildings, muddy walkways, and filthy sanitary conditions." However, now, the federal government had an official presence on the ground and began to force some order on what had still been, in many respects, a frontier town. Before the fire, a variety of private businesses were jammed among the bathhouses along Valley Street (now Central Avenue), but after the fire, the government set aside the eastern side of the street to be the exclusive domain of bathing facilities, thus creating Bathhouse Row. Moreover, potential bathhouse builders had to submit their architectural plans to the secretary of the interior for approval, and a variety of strict regulations for bathhouse operations were instituted. According to Shugart, "Between 1879 and 1895 the rough frontier town was transformed into an elegant spa city with palatial, world-class hotels and a lively social season."[53]

Although the federal government could control bathhouse operations, it had little control over the city's more illicit activities. By the late 1870s, there were twenty saloons in the downtown area, with many having gambling operations on the second floor.[54] Despite the intention of the petitioners for the incorporation of Hot Springs to limit the influence of undesirables, Hot Springs in the years immediately following incorporation was a rough and rowdy place—but its reputation was often due as much to the deeds of its own city leaders as it was to any "undesirables." For example, on November 15, 1877, T.F. Linde, a dentist then serving both as mayor and chief of police, was accused by Charles Matthews, editor of the *Hot Springs Daily Hornet*, of not enforcing local laws against gambling. When Linde encountered Matthews on what is now Central Avenue, he pulled out a pistol and began firing wildly at the editor, who, despite being hit three times, was able to wrest the gun from his attacker. Thereupon, Linde pulled out a second gun and began firing wildly again, in the process injuring a street peddler and a city councilman. This behavior, however, did not result in his removal from office; in fact, at the conclusion of his trial in nearby Benton (having been relocated from Garland County) on September 24, 1879, Linde was fined a total of $105 and sentenced to ten minutes in the county jail.[55] Matthews later waged a war of words against a trio of locally powerful men known as the Arlington Gang: Dewitt C. Rugg, then part owner of the Arlington Hotel; businessman Samuel W. Fordyce, also part owner of the Arlington; and saloon operator Frank Flynn, who had a gambling club in the Arlington. Specifically, Matthews alleged that Rugg and Fordyce had bribed former U.S. senator Stephen Wallace Dorsey to secure a lease on the government ground on which the Arlington was built. On September 22, 1882, Fordyce confronted Matthews and began beating the newspaperman with a club before trying to shoot him. Rugg and Flynn quickly showed up during this contest and also began shooting at Matthews, who was struck dead. Rugg and Flynn were acquitted of manslaughter, while the charge against Fordyce was reduced to assault and battery, and he was fined $200 for his role in the affair.[56]

Fordyce had come to Hot Springs in 1873 for health-related reasons, having suffered numerous injuries and malaria during his service for the

Union in the Civil War, but returned later that decade with an eye toward developing the town, investing in various bathhouses, hotels and public services, in addition to building railroads in and beyond Arkansas. At his death in 1919, the *Arkansas Gazette* opined that he "was one of the empire builders, one of the men whose vision, energy and ability have made America."[57] Aiding in the murder of a newspaper editor apparently did not diminish his reputation in the slightest.

Two years later, there occurred what became known later as the Flynn-Doran War, a battle between Frank Flynn, the local boss who oversaw all gambling operations in the city, and Major S. Alex Doran, a former Confederate officer who had reopened two clubs previously abandoned by one of Flynn's would-be competitors. Each side armed itself for the inevitable conflict, which occurred on February 9, 1884, when the Doran gang attacked a buggy in which Frank Flynn was riding with his brothers William (Billy) and John—right on Central Avenue in downtown Hot Springs. The Doran gang succeeded in killing three people, including Frank Hall (the driver of the carriage) and Billy and John Flynn, as well as wounding Frank Flynn and two bystanders. As the *Arkansas Gazette* reported, "The firing continued for several minutes, during which time buckshot and pistol balls rained up and down the avenue in murderous numbers." Thomas Toler, the chief of police, quickly arrested the seven members of the Doran gang, placing himself in the midst of the firefight, though the initial *Gazette* report also indicated the possibility of some members of the police being involved with the Doran gang, as one Detective Danto was arrested in connection with the shooting.[58] A group dubbed the Citizens' Committee rounded up three "imported desperadoes and members of the Flynn gang" and ordered them to leave town. In this, they were backed up by Chief Toler. However, Sheriff J.H. Nichols interfered to protect the members of the Flynn gang and also tried to claim the charge of the Doran men.[59] A company of militia was organized to patrol Hot Springs and keep the peace in the wake of the violence, and with the backing of the militia, a much larger Citizens' Committee later that month once again rounded up the three men and placed them on the morning train out of the city.[60]

Soon after their arrest, the accused found themselves represented by some of the state's most prestigious lawyers, who put forward a claim of self-defense.[61] On February 21, charges were dismissed against two of the Doran party.[62] The remainder were acquitted in the first trial, for the murder of Frank Hall, in early May, and the remaining cases were postponed to the next session of the court.[63] In the end, Doran himself went free, being acquitted of the final charge against him in March 1886, although a report on the matter demonstrated either astonishing naivete or irresponsible idealism when it declared: "To the intense relief of the people of Hot Springs the matter has been definitely and finally settled in the courts, and the city is becoming rapidly short of the bad influences which led to all the trouble."[64] The conflict between the two parties, however, continued, even if it did not break out into such overwhelming violence, until July 16, 1887, when Doran was shot down elsewhere by a man—and, yes, this was his real name, as reported in the newspapers—known as Pink Fagg.[65] This left the Flynn faction in charge of gambling in the Spa City.

The 1880s saw more than violence, for trolley lines had been laid down, as had gas and water lines, and an archway over Hot Springs Creek had been completed, thus helping with the flooding that regularly plagued the downtown area. Economic growth proceeded apace, with new hotels, a packing company, a steam laundry and more being established in the coming years. But not all the new business was exactly legitimate. Befitting its Wild West reputation, Hot Springs had long featured brothels, but in the 1890s, their operations became more brazen, with one local madam, Josie Belmont, publicly listing her occupation in the 1897 city directory as "madam."[66] In addition, a number of gambling clubs opened up for the entertainment of locals and visitors alike. Perhaps the most famous, the Southern Club, was built in 1893 by Charles Dugan and Dan Stuart, although it was later taken over by Sam Watt, a nephew of longtime Garland County sheriff Robert L. Williams (about whom more will shortly be said). By the early twentieth century, Hot Springs would be home to a number of gambling clubs—the Ohio Club, the Kentucky Club, the Indiana Club, the Arkansas Club, the Texas Club and the West End Club, among many others.[67] However, despite the reputation these clubs would justly gain for being violent and disturbing influences on the community, the law itself could be more violent.

"Five Men Shot to Death; Pandemonium at Hot Springs"—thus read the headline of the March 17, 1899 *Arkansas Gazette*, but just who was shot to death made this affair more than the usual exemplar of lawlessness in the Spa City, for the dead included chief of police Thomas C. Toler, sergeant of police Tom Goslee, city detective James E. Hart, businessman Louis Hinkle and John O. Williams, the son of Sheriff Robert L. Williams. However, it was no criminal syndicate that snuffed out the lives of these men, for the main combatants were the Hot Springs Police Department and the Garland County Sheriff's Office.[68]

Chief Toler had been reappointed by Mayor William L. Gordon in 1897, but the two soon clashed on a fundamental matter. As Allbritton has written, "Gordon was more conservative than Toler, who wanted to see the city 'open-up more,' or at least have a liberal view of the type of entertainment many visitors sought. Under the liberal view, the gambling and prostitution elements would be regulated and fined, bringing in money to the city coffers."[69] Gordon tried to dismiss his permissive police chief, but the city council backed Toler, and come the next election, Toler threw his support behind independent candidate C.W. Fry, who managed one of the bathhouses and had promised to reappoint Toler. However, the county sheriff, Robert L. Williams, threw his support behind Democratic candidate George Belding, a local businessman, who promised to appoint the sheriff's brother, Coffey Williams, to the position of police chief—which would have given the Williams clan control of law enforcement in both the city and the county. On March 16, the chief of police held a political caucus for Fry in his office at city hall. Word of this, including a list of attendees (many of whom were Hot Springs police officers), quickly made its way back to Sheriff Williams. Williams was walking down the street with a friend, Dave Young, when he caught sight of Sergeant Tom Goslee, whose name was on the list of attendees. The sheriff confronted Goslee about the matter, and things grew heated between the men before Young stepped in to separate them and Goslee went his own way. Williams turned toward the City Hall Saloon, where he met his son, John, who passed him a .44 pistol. Later, each side would accuse the other of initiating the fight, but however it started, Bob and John Williams were soon emptying their revolvers at Goslee, who fired back with his derringer before fleeing unharmed.

Later, at city hall, Goslee relayed his story to prosecuting attorney David M. Cloud, who issued a warrant for the arrest of the sheriff. Williams was arrested and made bail, but as Allbritton notes, Toler "recognized a volatile situation existed" and aimed to try to patch things up with the sheriff, sending Goslee to meet John Williams and do likewise.[70] The sheriff sent his brother Coffey to accompany John to the meeting with Goslee, and they were soon joined by Deputy Ed Spear. When the trio encountered Goslee, Toler and Captain Lee Haley, Goslee and John Williams shook hands and began joking. Haley and Spear moved over to Lemps Beer Depot, where they ended up in an argument in which Spear seemed to imply that the bartender (and brother-in-law of Haley), Lewis Hinkle, was a liar. Hinkle responded by grabbing Spear and slashing his throat with a six-inch knife. Haley tried to separate the men, and Spear managed to twist free and fire at Hinkle as the other actors converged on the same spot. Coffey Williams shot Hinkle dead. John Williams shot and wounded Goslee, who turned and killed him before being shot mortally, in turn, by Coffey Williams. Police Chief Toler fired at both Spear and Williams but was struck down by them. Sheriff Robert Williams arrived on the scene to find his son dead, and his rage grew to the point where, when Detective James E. Hart later showed up, he fired into the face of the man known widely as "Uncle Jim," despite the officer's complete lack of connection to the affair.

It was an hour before city police arrived to restore order and clear away the bodies—and they only showed up because local businesses called city hall to complain. As soon as what passed for order was restored, many of "the more timid visitors" began leaving the city.[71] Despite the evidence against Sheriff Williams, especially for the murder of Hart, who did not have his gun drawn (as witnesses readily testified), trial after trial of the man ended in a hung jury before resolution was achieved—though, as Allbritton notes, "It was not the finest hour of the Garland County Circuit Court when a jury finally returned a 'not guilty' verdict."[72] Williams's life afterward was shrouded in controversy, including allegations of election tampering and indictments for murder and nonfeasance. He was occasionally reelected sheriff before his 1917 suicide. And the effects of the shootout lingered for years: "It became necessary for the business community to spend large amounts of money advertising on how safe the Spa had become."[73]

Safe or not, Hot Springs regularly advertised itself as the cure for a variety of ills, perhaps specializing in the treatment of what was then called neurasthenia. A term coined by neurologist George Beard in 1869, neurasthenia was primarily identified as a nervous disorder affecting those whose brains were most preoccupied with the busy mechanisms that sustained modern life—what might today be termed *burnout*. According to historian Elliot G. Bowen, the proper approach to neurasthenia was not medical in nature but, rather, entailed a "rest cure, and the southern states—due, no doubt, not only to climate but also to a perception about the more relaxed pace of life below the Mason-Dixon line—became the destinations of choice for well-heeled urbanites of the north suffering this particular disorder."[74] People were already venturing to Hot Springs for the reported curative powers of its waters, and by the 1890s, as local business elites began to pour money into the development of bathhouses and the construction of hotels, the city began to acquire a national reputation as a treatment center for the wealthy who were nervously exhausted by lives of overwork and overconsumption.[75] Not only did the regimen of bathing on

Army Navy Hospital in Hot Springs. *Courtesy of Hot Springs National Park.*

offer at Hot Springs require significant periods of rest, but the location of the city—in the remote Ouachita Mountains of Arkansas, within a state still structurally underdeveloped at the time—essentially cut the individual off from the concourse of modern society for the period of his or her treatment. This is not to say, however, that visitors were cut off from luxury, for the growing number of hotels offered a range of enticements and services.

Care was extended not just to the overworked middle class but also to veterans of the military. Following the Civil War, as historian Fred Cron has written, "the sick and wounded from both armies poured into Hot Springs, hoping to recover the health they had lost in the rigors of campaigning."[76] Many were impoverished and resorted to a series of makeshift pools that were little more than holes dug into the ground. A local physician, Algernon S. Garnett, led an effort for the establishment of a national hospital for veterans, and the idea gained steam after Senator John A. Logan, a Union veteran and member of the Grand Army of the Republic, visited the city in 1882. The Army and Navy General Hospital, as it was designated, constituted a Swiss chalet–type construction, built between 1884 and 1886; given that it was built on federal land, only Union veterans were permitted access. It opened to patients on January 7, 1887, and though the residents of Hot Springs were certainly proud to have such an important national structure located in their community, it did occasionally constitute a source of friction. As Cron notes, "Many of the army medical officers were frankly skeptical of the curative powers of the water, and such heresy was a sure cause of unpopularity in Hot Springs in those days."[77] The current brick building that replaced the original in 1933 is perhaps the most prominent structure in the physical landscape of the city.

People of the lower classes were also provided for at Hot Springs. Various indigents had taken to camping around a site known as Ral Hole, called that perhaps because it was said to treat neuralgia (specific curative powers were often attributed to specific springs). After the Department of the Interior appointed him as the first superintendent at Hot Springs in 1877, Benjamin F. Kelly issued an order to those at what was now dubbed Ral City to vacate the area, and he built the first Government Free Bathhouse for indigent bathers away from the main section of Bathhouse Row. However, the water tended to be cold by the time it made its way to the free bathhouse, and many ended up back on the mountain at their improvised holes. After the 1878 fire, more indigents found their way to the free bathing site up the mountain, and ongoing conflict between indigents and those who possessed a vision of Hot Springs that catered to the more refined carried on through the end of the year, until Congress intervened and passed legislation requiring the construction and maintenance of free bathhouses for the poor. Ral Hole was sealed up, and a new Government Free Bathhouse was constructed over a spring colloquially known as the Mud Hole.

The building was never equal to the demand, and its shoddy construction became a source of shame for the emerging spa destination, and so the Government Free Bathhouse building was replaced in 1891. An 1898 expansion provided superintendent William Lee the opportunity to remodel the building to allow for racial segregation, breaking up the interior into four quadrants to separate it along both racial and gender lines.[78] But the free bathhouse would, for the duration of its existence, remain a point of contention, especially for the operators of the other bathhouses, who claimed that it "stole" potential paying customers.

From the 1890s on through the 1940s, the name of Hot Springs was associated nationally with the disease of syphilis due to the fact that thousands of people each year ventured to the Arkansas community to seek treatment for their malady, earning the city the title of "Mecca for syphilitics in America." As Bowen writes, "Hot Springs in many ways functioned as the medical epicenter of America's pre-penicillin encounter with syphilis."[79] While treatment of syphilis during this time consisted of varying measures of moral reform and scientific method, Bowen

The first free bathhouse in Hot Springs. *Courtesy of Hot Springs National Park.*

found a different ethos of treatment being practiced in Arkansas's spa city, where "resident medical men consistently approached syphilis as if it was a byproduct of modern life, something whose cure and control required not only drugs, but also a remedy that functioned as an antidote to civilization."[80] This sensibility, Bowen asserts, stemmed from the city's status as a health resort. In the late 1800s, Americans traveled in droves to such rural resorts in order to escape urban environments increasingly seen as "disease-ridden" and fundamentally unhealthy, to both mind and body, in the post–Civil War years; the "environment" of the countryside was regarded as the antidote to what historian Charles Rosenberg had dubbed the "pathologies of progress."[81]

Medical professionals in Hot Springs, in the postwar years, worked to attract syphilitics to the city, believing the thermal waters could offer relief, and by the late 1800s, word about the treatment being offered there had begun to make its way into medical journals and even newspapers. The treatment offered in the bathhouses of Hot Springs—which included repeated sessions of immersion in the scalding hot waters, as well as drinking the spring water, followed by a resting period in a cooling room—offered, at best, only a temporary respite from the ravages of the disease, even when augmented with mercurial ointments and other contemporary, pre-antibiotic medicines. However, at a time when major hospitals and many in private practice were actively shunning people infected with syphilis, at least Hot Springs offered, if not necessarily a respite from the physical ailment, a lack of condemnation and even a sense of hope for men and women who, otherwise, were left to endure the disease alone. While some syphilitics either sought treatment under assumed identities due to the shame associated with the disease or tried to hide their diagnoses altogether, "most syphilitics treated this city as the one place they did not have to disguise the reality of their venereal sicknesses."[82] One holdout against this welcoming approach was the Army and Navy General Hospital in Hot Springs, which, through the year 1910, "implemented a series of measures designed to prevent the admittance of venereally-afflicted soldiers and sailors." In 1910, however, this ban was rescinded, and the introduction of the Wassermann test around the same time meant that this federal institution became yet another important Hot Springs site for the treatment of syphilis and similar diseases.[83]

Increased competition among those selling healthcare services led some physicians and hotel proprietors, as the city rose to national prominence in the late nineteenth century, to hire "drummers." As local historian Mary D. Hudgins explains, "The epithet indicated an individual who made his living touting unsuspecting individuals come to the resort for the first time to specific physicians, hotels, boarding houses, bath houses and sometimes even drug stores. Superficially the custom doesn't seem particularly reprehensible. But as carried on, it became definitely predatory."[84] Proprietors would pay these drummers a set fee for each visitor directed their way. During Mayor Linde's first term, the city declared the practice illegal and set fines for violations, but this did not curtail drumming, and later, the city decided to try licensing the practice. However, nothing seemed to make drumming less obnoxious, and soon drummers were taking the train to nearby Malvern or Little Rock to target those traveling to Hot Springs before they even arrived in the city. "Staff members from the office of Hot Springs Reservation," writes Hudgins, "were designated to board trains and pass out leaflets telling of hot springs facilities, and warning newcomers against being taken in by strangers recommending specific physicians and hotels."[85] By the early twentieth century, these drummers "were so numerous that they themselves became a nuisance by their sheer numbers. At times they gathered so thickly about pullmans and chair cars that it was difficult for passengers to descend to the platform."[86] Efforts by

Baseball players during spring training in Hot Springs. *Courtesy of Hot Springs National Park.*

federal authorities, the Business Men's League, railroad companies and a group of concerned citizens dubbed the Visitors' Protective Association helped stem the practice, and drumming eventually faded.

For several decades, a number of major league baseball teams conducted spring training (no pun intended) at Hot Springs. In 1886, the National League's Chicago White Stockings (forerunner of the Chicago Cubs) became the first team to venture south for spring training; Hot Springs was chosen not only for the warmer climate but also for the baths, which would give players a chance to "boil out the alcoholic microbes."[87] The team apparently played on a field near the present-day courthouse, and the experiment in spring training seemed to pay off when the White Stockings won the pennant later that year, so they returned the following year. In 1890, teams from Chicago, Buffalo, Cleveland and Denver trained in Hot Springs.[88] Others soon came, though managers often had difficulty ensuring that players did not spend their nights among the city's various attractions, such as women, saloons and gambling—although sometimes managers themselves partook of the delights of the city, as was the case with "Mugsy" McGraw, manager of the New York Giants, who was arrested in 1894 for gambling.[89] The men of the major league regularly played demonstration games that attracted large audiences, thus increasing the allure of the Spa City. Of course, the most famous of these visitors to the city was Babe Ruth, who arrived in 1915, still early in his major league career, and like many of his fellow players, he not only trained but also enjoyed the recreational opportunities afforded, especially the golfing.

Many of these players also enjoyed the horse races available in Hot Springs. As Allbritton has written, "For a period of time in the late 1800s, the Spa had boasted of two small tracks which had lured hundreds of sporting and betting people to the city. Neither of these two tracks, Sportsman Park and Coombs Track, were destined to greatness and only scant records remain of their existence."[90] In 1903, however, one "Umbrella Bill" McGuigan of Garland County, elected the previous year to the Arkansas House of Representatives, introduced a bill to repeal state anti-racing laws. As it happened, he owned a tract of flat land along Gulpha Creek, and on February 25, 1904, Essex Park opened for business there. Although still under construction, it drew a crowd estimated at five thousand, and as the *Arkansas Gazette* reported, "Many of the largest betting operators in the entire United States are on hand, while a number of high class horses are here."[91] Less than a year later, on February 15, 1905, Oaklawn Park opened.[92]

Oaklawn eventually outdid Essex, and the latter was forced to cancel its 1906 racing season. McGuigan had previously sold his holdings in Essex Park, but with a clause that mandated ownership revert to him should horse racing not continue at the site for five years. Perhaps seeking some revenge against Oaklawn, the one-term state representative, in 1907, managed to get state senator Walter S. Amis to expand his bill against pool halls to include any and all gambling.[93] The bill saw stiff resistance in the Arkansas Senate, even being subjected to a filibuster, before it was finally signed into law on February 27, 1907.[94] Once the law went into effect, local authorities forbade the presence of bookmakers and betters at Oaklawn. The management of Oaklawn continued to run races "as a free exercise of its corporate functions, free from interference," and warned people not to treat the park "as a gambling house," as the company held out to test the new law in the courts.[95] In the face of this, a group of local citizens formed the Citizens Improvement Union, "whose function it was to oversee closing public gambling houses that operated in Hot Springs in flagrant violation of the Amis Bill," according to local historian Isabel Burton Anthony. This went beyond the racetracks: "The Kentucky Club, Ohio, Illinois and Texas Bar Clubs, the Little Casino and Bryan's Saloon faced sanctions by Gen. B. W. Green, commander in chief of the state militia, who was sent to Hot Springs from Little Rock representing the governor."[96] The union even considered action against Oaklawn's original charter, while a grand jury reported back that the law was being violated at Oaklawn. Finally, on March 30, 1907, Oaklawn closed its doors, cutting short its racing season.[97] It would be a decade before racing returned to Hot Springs.

On February 25, 1905, at around three o'clock in the morning, the Grand Central Hotel, about a block from Central Avenue, caught fire for reasons that remain undetermined. Although hotel guests were able to evacuate due to the quick thinking of the watchman and night clerk, the fire spread and soon engulfed the neighboring Methodist church. Strong winds spread the flames to more and more buildings, driving the fire in the direction of the county courthouse and jail. The fire department had succeeded in bringing the blaze under control by around five o'clock in the morning, but then the water pressure suddenly gave out, and firefighters quickly organized a bucket brigade with civilians, many still in their pajamas. The county sheriff was able to move the prisoners from the jail and save the city's tax records, but numerous buildings—including the county courthouse, Quapaw School, several businesses and residential buildings—were consumed by the fire. By the time it was extinguished around nine thirty that morning, the fire had claimed more than two dozen lives and one hundred acres of property in downtown Hot Springs.[98] Reports in the *Arkansas Gazette* counted as many as two thousand people homeless and forty blocks destroyed for a possible total of $2 million in damages (or approximately $67 million in 2022 dollars); regardless, it easily constituted "the greatest fire in Arkansas history." Firefighters had even dynamited buildings in order to prevent the spread of fire northward into the valley. By the next day, sightseers arrived en masse to gaze at the damage and pick through the ruins for souvenirs, but Mayor George Belding was, by all accounts, ably leading the work in salvaging and rebuilding, with the *Gazette* reporting "that so much order as prevailed could have been brought out of so much chaos in so short a time is remarkable."[99]

After this fire, the architecture of Hot Springs began to change, with stone and brick buildings replacing the cheaper wooden structures. Among these was the Garland County Courthouse. The cornerstone was laid on August 15, 1905, and the new building was completed the following year, designed in a Neoclassical Revival style and constructed of brick. The building included fireproof vaults designed to keep county records safe.[100] And here, there would occur a drama that would, in many ways, set the stage for the murder of Oscar Chitwood.

In large, bold font, the *Sentinel Record* of January 26, 1910, exclaimed, "Negro Brute Attempts an Assault on School Girl."[101] The day before, ten-year-old Lena Adams was walking to her grandmother's house on Summer

Street from Oaklawn School along a rarely used path through south Hot Springs over Stoake's Creek when a "youthful brown negro man or boy" blocked her way.[102] Adams recognized him as the same person who had repeatedly attempted to entice her with gifts along the path on several previous days, but on this morning, he was reportedly far more aggressive and, after a failed attempt to lure her with the promise of a rooster for her mother, eventually "put one black hand across her mouth, another around her waist and dragged her from the roadway." Adams fought back, "frightened at the manner of the negro." The assailant, according to one account, took her to "a little negro hut" that he claimed to inhabit, and there he "laid her down."[103]

As Adams struggled to resist her attacker, Ella Kariger and M.E. Grimstead, visitors to Hot Springs from Kansas, heard "a stifled noise" that interrupted their walk. They walked toward the sound until the attacker looked up at them. The ladies saw a second figure under the attacker, and at first, they thought the second person was "a little negro boy" and that they had interrupted a wrestling match. At that moment, Adams rose, exposing her white, female face, and "the women screamed for help." The attacker fled through the woods, while the women took Adams to a nearby home, where she gave a full account of the incident.

The *Sentinel Record* published a detailed description of the unidentified attacker, based on information from Adams. He was "a brown skinned negro" with a "medium build" weighing roughly 140 pounds. He was about seventeen or eighteen years of age. The newspaper explained that "his features are not those of the distinct negro type." He had neither "thick lips" nor a "flat nose" but instead possessed "thin lips and very ordinary features." The assailant wore a dark cap with a button on the front, a dark coat and light pants, which were soiled at the knees. The attacker also had a small dog with him that looked like a rat terrier with white fur dotted with two yellow spots.

Garland County sheriff Jake Houpt gathered his deputies and began scouring the area where Adams was attacked, and Hot Springs city police chief Frank Moore assigned all available officers to the case. Early in the evening, several "negro suspects were picked up," but when police brought the suspects to Adams, "she assured the officers that neither one was the man," and the police released them. Men from the community quickly gathered, armed themselves with an arsenal of "shotguns, Winchester rifles, six shooters, and other forms of weapons," and joined the search. The newspaper claimed there was no mob violence and no frantic outpouring of emotions. Instead, men formed small teams and were soon "quietly and separately working about the south part of the city" in hopes that they would "trap the black demon [who] for lust who would make such an attempt on a little child."[104]

A rumor circulated among the vigilantes early on the morning of January 26 that an unnamed "negro porter" who worked at the Lyceum Theatre might be the assailant. Workers at the Lyceum Theatre told reporters that the man could not have attacked Adams, since he was at work at the time of the attack. Four armed men did not bother to inform law enforcement and took matters into their own hands, arriving at the man's house and taking him away. The man's sister was worried because her brother was quietly "taken into the woods" by the four vigilantes and had not returned. The police stated that they knew nothing about the woman's brother.[105] The newspaper said nothing more about the unnamed man, and it is unclear if he ever returned from the woods.

The police soon announced that they were looking for but had not yet apprehended a young man named Harry Poe. A young boy who had spent the night at the same home as Poe the night before informed police that Poe had borrowed his cap, which matched the description of the cap worn by the attacker, on the day of the attack and returned it that evening. The police took the cap as evidence. The police received information that Poe worked at Cooper's stable. The supervisor at the stable informed police that Poe did not work there, but the police found a dog matching the description of the attacker's dog at the stable and took the dog as evidence. The police believed that the confiscation of the cap and dog would help them identify the attacker.[106]

On January 27, the *Sentinel-Record* informed readers that officers, sheriff's deputies and one hundred "voluntary aids" had scoured the countryside. Two men were under arrest in the city jail, awaiting possible identification by Lena Adams. Meanwhile, residents worried about "the fact that a negro fiend was at large." Rumors of a race riot on Third Street spread, and police rushed to the scene only to find an unspecified "quiet co-operative movement," which was no cause for alarm. Reports also circulated through the city that "some negroes had planned to make an attack on the jail" and free the suspects under arrest, but the *Sentinel-Record* comforted the city's residents that "negro outlaws who might attempt such an action would be few."[107] By January 27, word of the attack on Adams and the bands of heavily armed vigilantes had spread to Little Rock. A writer for the *Arkansas Gazette* predicted that "should the fugitive be located, little doubt is expressed but that he will be shot by members of the posse."[108] Rumors circulated through town that the man who attacked Adams had already fled Garland County, but members of law enforcement were adamant that escape was impossible and that they were on the verge of bringing the "fiend" to justice, whoever it might be.[109]

Prosecuting attorney Henry B. Means requested a warrant for Harry Poe's arrest, and Garland County justice of the peace Thomas Gladson signed the warrant.[110] On January 27, relatives of Harry Poe surrendered him to authorities. According to reports, they explained that Poe was innocent of attacking Adams and had evaded arrest because he was guilty of attempting "to assault an old negro woman."[111] Poe's relatives were worried that the vigilantes would murder him if they found him before the police did.[112] Sheriff Jake Houpt loaded Harry Poe in an open buggy and took him to the home of Lena Adams. According to the *Sentinel-Record*, Adams said, "[H]ere comes the negro now," as Poe came into view. Houpt next took Poe to see Kariger and Grimstead. Both ladies agreed that Poe was man who attacked Adams.[113]

Sheriff Houpt feared that the armed men roaming town might rush the jail and murder Poe before he could stand trial, so Deputy Reb Houpt and Hot Springs police lieutenant W.W. Willey escorted Poe to the train station, where they boarded a train to Little Rock with plans to take Poe to the state penitentiary. According to the *Arkansas Gazette* in Little Rock, thirty armed men, part of a larger crowd of up to one hundred people, arrived "intent upon getting possession of the negro."[114] The *Sentinel Record* in Hot Springs downplayed the potential violence at the depot, admitting that while "several were armed with Winchesters and shotguns," the crowd was peaceful, "most of them were attracted by curiosity" and there was "no vigorous attempt to take the negro from the officers." Five African Americans approached the depot and offered to help the authorities protect Poe. In response, "an officer turned the business end of a shotgun on them and kept them at a distance until the train had departed." Despite the armed crowd and potential for violence, Poe was stoic and "was not disposed to exhibit any fear if he felt any."[115] Authorities successfully transported Poe to Little Rock.

Under intense pressure to move quickly, Hot Springs chief of police Moore suggested convening a special session of the circuit court to try Poe rapidly and prevent vigilantes from murdering him.[116] This legal maneuver was permitted due to Act 258, passed by the Arkansas legislature the previous year. Act 258 stated that whenever a "rape, murder, or any other crime, calculated to arouse the passions of the people" was committed, the sheriff "shall notify the judge of the circuit or district" and request "a special term of the court in order that the person or persons charged with such a crime or crimes may be brought to immediate trial."[117]

On January 31, authorities brought Poe back to Hot Springs for a preliminary hearing to review the case.[118] Poe requested the assistance of a lawyer for the preliminary hearing, but justice of the peace Tom Gladson denied the request.[119] However, Poe was allowed to cross-examine at least two of the three witnesses. The court heard testimony from Lena Adams, Emma Grinstead and Ella Kariger.[120] Lena Adams testified that Poe approached her and "throwed me on the ground" when she refused to stop. She explained that he then pulled her underwear down, partially undressed himself and "laid down on me." Prosecuting attorney H.B. Means asked Adams if Poe hurt Adams "there," and Adams responded, "A little bit." Means also asked, "Do you know how he was hurting you there, do you know what he was hurting you with?" To this, Adams replied, "No."[121] This detail was important because under Arkansas law at the time, rape was defined as "penetration with the virile or male organ," although "in the case of rape of a female child perfect penetration is not necessary."[122] Gladson did not ask Poe if he wanted to cross-examine Adams. Poe might not have even been in the room when Adams testified, since "the court room was cleared" to "make it easier" for her.[123]

The two visitors from Kansas, Emma Grinstead and Ella Kariger, also testified at the preliminary hearing. Both ladies identified Poe as the man they saw attacking Adams and testified that Poe fled when he saw them. Grinstead testified that when she approached Adams, the girl's clothing was "disarranged," and her face and body were covered with "print marks of the fingers where he had held her." Ella Kariger gave similar testimony, stating that when they found Adams, "her clothing was badly disarranged" and "her face was all purple and red where he had strangled her." Poe asked Kariger, "What kind of clothes did I have on?" Kariger responded that he had "either a black coat or a dark blue one and gray pants, as to your cap I didn't notice." Poe fired back, "I haven't got any gray pants, nobody in the city ever seen me wear any gray pants of any kind."[124] Despite Poe's protests, Gladson found that there was sufficient evidence to hold Poe and convene a special grand jury.

Garland County authorities continued to play a deadly game of cat and mouse with the area's vigilantes. Sheriff Houpt received word, shortly after Poe attended his preliminary hearing, that "an organized movement" planned to ambush and murder Poe when authorities attempted to return him to Little Rock by train. Chief of police Moore distracted a crowd of armed men at the train station by giving them misleading information so that Poe could be slipped out of town.[125]

On February 5, attorney R.E.L. Maxey began work as Harry Poe's defense lawyer.[126] He first announced plans to request a change of venue. Maxey also moved to quash all evidence presented during the preliminary proceedings in which Poe did not enjoy the benefit of counsel. At least a few people in Hot Springs responded to Maxey's defense of Poe with "a revival of open revolt talk." A writer for the *Sentinel-Record* argued that "lynchings have taken place everywhere civilization exists for less than the crime in this case" and predicted that if the authorities did not execute Poe quickly, "there may be open revolt."[127] Indeed, tensions remained high in Hot Springs as the city prepared for Poe's trial. The *Sentinel-Record* reported that "there is said to be some feeling against" Robert Adams, who was the father of Lena Adams, because "he had opportunity to kill Poe and did not do so."[128] The press did not print a response from Robert Adams, only a comment that he was leaving town on business but planned to return for the trial.[129] A series of brief letters appeared in the *Sentinel-Record* urging "speedy justice in the Poe case" and arguing that "Poe must pay the penalty of his crime."[130] On February 24, the *Sentinel-Record* published an "appeal for the law" by S.E.J. Watson, the pastor of the Roanoke Baptist Church and president of the Colored Minister's Alliance. Watson urged the people of Hot Springs to "let Harry Poe come to justice," assuring readers that he and "every negro man who has the respect of his race" condemned "crime in any form."[131]

After several weeks of preparation, a Garland County grand jury indicted Harry Poe for the crime of rape.[132] The trial followed the indictment without pause. Consistent with earlier proceedings, the prosecution's case rested primarily on the testimony of Lena Adams, who "identified him positively" and "recited the story of her experiences in detail." Emma Grinstead and Ella Kariger had returned home, and thus, their testimony from the preliminary hearing was read into the record, without the defense being able to cross-examine either witness. Maxey tried to call several witnesses who were willing to testify that Poe was elsewhere at the time of the attack, but the judge refused to allow their testimony. Prosecutor Means used his closing statement for reciting "the peculiar horror of the crime" and "describing the revolting nature" of the incident. The jury found Poe guilty, and the court sentenced Poe to hang on April 1.[133]

Maxey immediately filed a motion for a new trial, listing several errors and irregularities that called into question the verdict, including the fact

Panoramic view of Hot Springs. *Courtesy of Library of Congress.*

that the court had denied Poe "the privilege to have his attorney present" at the preliminary hearing.[134] However, the Supreme Court of Arkansas ruled that Poe had, in fact, received a fair trial and that the evidence was sufficient to warrant the sentence of death.[135] Poe's attorney filed a petition for a rehearing, his client maintaining his innocence in the matter and apparently receiving support from an unnamed member of a "delegation of society women from Hot Springs" who called on the penitentiary to visit the young man.[136] Two white women, a Mrs. Woodcock and her daughter, Dora Velvin, visited Governor George Washington Donaghey with R.E.L. Maxey, who was still serving as Poe's lawyer, and "two negroes named Mitchell" to petition the governor for clemency. Woodcock firmly stated that, at the very time Poe had allegedly attacked Lena Adams, she had ventured to the house of Poe's mother, who did her laundry, to check on what had delayed the return of her clothing, and she saw Poe there. However, the court refused a rehearing on the technical grounds that the term of the trial court had passed.[137] With the execution date set for September 2, rumors began to circulate that Maxey had made plans to take Lena Adams to the governor's office to relay a different version of events for Governor Donaghey in a bid for executive clemency, and a committee of fifty citizens paid a visit to Maxey, "informing him that they did not come for purposes of intimidation, but that if he exceeded what would be expected of a lawyer in the premises, or if the child was disturbed, he would be made answerable personally to the populace."[138]

While Poe's supporters fought to save his life, Poe waited in the state penitentiary. Guards reported that Poe was a model prisoner who never gave them any trouble. They claimed he maintained an "air of indifference" and "seemed cheerful." When the guards asked him how he felt, Poe replied that he was "mighty tired of being locked up" and

would like to be outdoors again, if only for a few moments.[139] As the time of the execution neared, several "well-known residents of Hot Springs" had begun to believe in Poe's innocence, so much so that the governor acceded to the request of Sheriff Houpt to place a company of the National Guard in Hot Springs for the day of the execution "to prevent possible interference by sympathizers."[140] While Poe had supporters in Hot Springs, other residents were eager to see him hang. C.H. Broughton, a relative of Lena Adams, gave Sheriff Houpt a rope and asked Houpt to hang Poe with it. Houpt decided the rope was too short and declined to use it for Poe's execution, but he did keep it, possibly for use as backup.[141] One last appeal to the governor was turned down.[142]

As Poe reached the execution scaffold, the aforementioned Reverend Watson held a short service for Poe near the scaffold and "delivered a fervent prayer for the soul of the negro."[143] When asked for a final statement, Harry Poe told the press, "I have nothing more than what I have always said—that I am innocent of the crime, and that I do not believe such a crime was ever committed. I am going to hang for rape, but I am innocent of the charge. I will meet my accusers and those who say I am guilty at the judgment seat." The night before, Poe had asked Sheriff Houpt if the stockade around the gallows could be removed so that all could witness the noon execution, but, as the *Hot Springs Daily News* reported, "of course such a request could not be complied with according to state law." By ten in the morning, a crowd of five hundred had gathered around the courthouse in anticipation, though only a select twenty-five were permitted to witness the execution.[144] Poe died on the gallows. The place and manner of his burial are unknown.

The scaffold on which Poe was hanged still stood on the night that Oscar Chitwood was murdered, several months later. And curiously, the rope that the family friend of Lena Adams had supplied the sheriff, asking that it be used for Poe's execution, would be found near the dead body of Chitwood.

CHAPTER 3

"I WAS NOT A BAD MAN"

I wrote the sheriff that I was not a bad man, that if he had a warrant for me I would come in and give myself up.... We went inside and had waited several minutes when the Houpts rushed in, grabbed George and said they had a warrant for him. They handled him rough and I became mad and drew my gun and backed them off. Then we rushed out and were untying our horses when they rushed out and commenced firing.

—*Statement of Oscar Chitwood published in the* Sentinel-Record[145]

The sun rose clear and bright over Hot Springs on August 17, 1910. From the windows of his second-floor office in the Garland County Courthouse on Ouachita Avenue, Sheriff Jake Houpt surveyed his domain. The Houpt family, along with their rivals the Williamses, dominated the county sheriff's office for nearly three decades, and Jake Houpt carried out his duties with the help of his brothers. Jake's younger brother, Sid Houpt, served as his chief deputy.[146] Reb Houpt, who served as sheriff from 1892 until 1898 when a court removed him from office for corruption, also served as a deputy. Jake's third brother, Henry Houpt, spent most of his time on the family farm but also helped as a part-time deputy.[147]

In July 1910, Jake Houpt won a hotly contested race for the Democratic Party's nomination for a second term as sheriff, which both reflected and further secured his position as a major political leader in the county. He would face a general election in November, but he had little to fear in the

Above: Garland County Courthouse in Hot Springs. *Courtesy of Christopher Thrasher.*

Right: Sheriff Jake Houpt and his wife. *Courtesy of Garland County Historical Society.*

Egbert Houpt and Elizabeth Williams Children circa 1910
L to R Back Row: Egbert Calvin "Cal" Houpt; Jacob Davis "Jake" Houpt; Henry Sabine Houpt;
Middle Row: Sarah Jacinthe Houpt Rutherford; Albert Cyrus "Bud" Houpt; Elizabeth Williams Houpt (seated in wheelchair); Relisman "Reb" Houpt; Mary Leah "Lee" Houpt Tate;
Front Row: Lela Neal "Lil" Houpt Reynolds and Sidney Roswell Houpt

Houpt family. Jake Houpt is second from the left in the back row. *Courtesy of Garland County Historical Society.*

democratic stronghold of Hot Springs.[148] Houpt's opponent in the 1910 primary, T.J. Richards, had accused the Houpt family and their supporters of rigging the election, but the courts rejected all claims of fraud and confirmed Houpt's victory.[149] Nobody was ever convicted of rigging the 1910 primary election, but there were reasons to doubt the legitimacy of Houpt's victory in the conflicted city of Hot Springs.[150]

On the morning of August 17, Jake Houpt received reports that Oscar and George Chitwood were seen drinking at saloons in Hot Springs the night before and had spent the night at Williams' Wagon Yard, within a few steps of the courthouse. A.H. Abraham, the sheriff of nearby Clark County, asked for Houpt's help apprehending the Chitwood brothers, who were wanted for stealing cattle and horses from a farmer just outside Amity,

Arkansas, about thirty miles southwest of Hot Springs. Jake asked his brother Sid to locate the Chitwoods and bring them to his office.[151]

By 1910, Oscar and George went by the last name Chitwood, but it was not their birth name. Rumor had it that they were originally known as the Smiths, but in 1900, they used the name Wright and lived in Lincoln Township in western Garland County with their widowed mother, Arvine; their brothers Andrew, Osa, Reuben and Jessie; and their sister Mahla.[152] It is not clear when the brothers started using the name Chitwood, but according to rumor, they took it from Dr. Joel Chitwood, who helped raise them and gave them a chance to go to school. Both brothers refused to study and allegedly turned to a life of crime. Oscar returned to Arkansas in May 1910 after spending several years stealing horses in Texas and reportedly serving time in the Texas penitentiary.[153] It is impossible to know with certainty if it the same person, but someone named Oscar Wright, matching the general description of the man later known as Oscar Chitwood, did plead guilty to theft in east Texas and was incarcerated at the state prison from June 6, 1907, to May 6, 1909.[154] George Chitwood had worked on a logging crew, but by 1910, his only occupation was selling illegal moonshine whiskey. The brothers were well-known "mountaineers" who "led a wild, reckless life, and were feared generally." Neighbors described the Chitwood family as "desperate and law defying."[155] A journalist in Little Rock dismissively described Oscar and George as "typical Arkansas mountaineers."[156]

Ted Ownby argued that southern men are forever torn between the competing ideals of the praying South, rooted in the pacifistic morality of the Second Great Awakening, and the hedonistic or fighting South of the barroom, sporting arena and battlefield. In the South, "the opposites of aggressive, fun-loving male impulses and a deep evangelical piety worked to intensify each other." Preachers belched fire and brimstone from their pulpits, and "when southerners sinned, they sinned with a vengeance."[157]

Hot Springs was, and remains, a physical manifestation of that conflict. Like most southern towns, Hot Springs was home to numerous churches that preached the values of temperance, chastity and pacificism. Unlike most southern towns, it was also home to numerous brothels, gambling dens and bars. For over a century, Hot Springs was a wide-open city where many members of law enforcement were happy to protect illicit businesses in exchange for cash and political support. Members of the Houpt family who served in law enforcement walked a fine line between their pews at the First Methodist Church and the back doors of illicit businesses. Of the three Houpt brothers who served as sheriff, two were eventually convicted of corruption and removed from office. The third was found guilty of illegally mishandling county property shortly after he was murdered.[158] While the Houpts may have looked at rough mountaineers like the Chitwood brothers with moralistic disdain, the Chitwoods later refused to surrender the moral high ground. Oscar Chitwood later argued, "I am not a desperado" and insisted he was "not a bad man."[159]

Sid Houpt entered the Williams' Wagon Yard and immediately recognized the Chitwood brothers based on A.H. Abraham's description. Both Chitwood brothers were less than five and a half feet tall and had blond hair. A Hot Springs journalist described the brothers as having "a feminine appearance for boys." They were not boys, but they were much younger than the Houpt brothers. Oscar was twenty-seven years old, and George was twenty-one. Perhaps to make up for their otherwise nonthreatening appearance, both Chitwood brothers dressed like "the characters written in novel form of the bravado days of the early west."[160] Each man wore western-style clothing, including peaked Tom Mix–style cowboy hats and bandanas around their necks. Each man also carried a .38 revolver on his hip. Sid Houpt approached the Chitwoods and said, "Boys, Jake wants to see you at his office." One of the brothers replied, "We'll be over in a few minutes," and Houpt left to await their arrival.[161] It is unclear why the brothers agreed to meet the sheriff in his office or what they might have discussed as they led their horses toward the courthouse. According to one contemporary commentator, the Chitwoods "had weighed the situation well before and were ready for any situation."[162]

The Chitwoods hitched their horses near the northeastern corner of the courthouse, entered the courthouse through the north door and climbed the stairs to the sheriff's second-floor office. The Chitwoods found Sid and Jake Houpt chatting with county clerk Robert Mooney and lawyer Erbert Rutherford. The "feminine," youthful, blond-haired Chitwood brothers in their rough cowboy-style dress stood in stark contrast with the older, dark-haired, thickly mustached Houpt brothers, who wore modern business suits, starched white shirts and bowties. The Chitwood brothers made no effort to conceal their revolvers from the unarmed lawmen. After exchanging pleasant greetings, one of the Chitwoods asked the sheriff pointedly, "What do you want with us?" Jake Houpt pulled out a slip of paper and replied, "I have a warrant for your arrest."[163] The time was ten o'clock.[164]

According to county clerk Mooney, both Chitwood brothers instantly pulled their revolvers. Sid Houpt took a step toward the gunmen, but Oscar Chitwood stopped him by saying, "Get back or I will kill you," as

Workers in an unidentified blacksmith shop in Hot Springs. *Courtesy of Butler Center for Arkansas Studies, Central Arkansas Library System.*

Movie star Tom Mix. The Chitwoods dressed in similar clothing, possibly in imitation of the famous movie star. *Courtesy of Library of Congress.*

he shoved him. Jake Houpt demanded to know whom Oscar Chitwood was talking to. Chitwood responded, "I am talking to you." The outlaws herded the Houpt brothers, Rutherford and Mooney down the hall toward the stairs. When they got within a few steps of the stairs, the Chitwood brothers broke away from their four prisoners, sprinted for the stairwell, bounded down to the first floor and ran out the front door. Jake Houpt returned to his office and emerged a moment later, his pistol in hand, and he ran down the stairs, just moments behind the Chitwoods. Sid Houpt did not even have a gun in the building but borrowed a pistol from the tax collector's office before following his brother.[165]

The lawmen caught up with the Chitwoods as the outlaws were untying their horses. Oscar Chitwood fired one round into the air, hoping to scare away the lawmen.[166] The Houpts were not deterred and advanced on the mountaineers. The Chitwoods opened fire on the Houpts, using their horses as cover. The Houpts were caught in the open with nothing between their bodies and the "fusillade of fire" that flew toward them. Despite the danger, the lawmen did not retreat or seek cover and returned fire with reckless disregard for their own safety. Sid Houpt, reportedly one of the finest shots in the county, fired a bullet that struck the heavy leather saddle of Oscar Chitwood's horse and frightened the animal without hurting it or either of the outlaws. A witness believed that Sid Houpt fired into the saddle on purpose in an effort to scare away the animal and convince the Chitwoods to surrender before someone got hurt.[167]

The Chitwoods mounted their horses and continued to fire as they spurred their mounts to a run. They might have gotten away, but unlike many roads in the county, Ouachita Avenue was paved, and metal horseshoes are not made for pavement. Oscar Chitwood's horse slipped and fell on the pavement, pinning Oscar and injuring his left foot.[168] A moment later, George's horse also slipped on the pavement, and George fell. As George hit the ground, he lost his grip on his pistol. Clerk Alf Whittington, who was near Sheriff Houpt but unarmed, yelled at the sheriff, "Now you can capture him, and won't have to kill him." Although both Chitwoods had threatened to kill the lawmen and fired at them, none of the bullets had hit anyone, and Whittington clearly thought that it still might be possible to arrest the outlaws without bloodshed.[169]

Jake Houpt rushed toward George Chitwood and yelled, "Hands up!" George Chitwood recovered his gun before Jake Houpt could reach him. For a moment, the lawman and the mountaineer stared each other down at gunpoint. Streetcar conductor J.F. Joplin, watching from a few feet away, described the stare down as "game man against game man." In the same moment, both George Chitwood and Jake Houpt fired their guns, and both men struck their targets. Witnesses were unsure which man had fired first.[170] George's bullet struck Jake under the arm, penetrating his lung, and the sheriff fell to the street, alive but badly wounded.[171] Jake's bullet hit George in the chest and penetrated downward into George's liver.[172]

George Chitwood staggered to a buggy tied up near the courthouse. He dropped his pistol once again and tried to untie the buggy. Before he could get away, Sid Houpt advanced on George and ordered him to surrender. The mountaineer did not say a word as he struck Sid Houpt over the head with the buggy's whip. Sid Houpt fired a single shot into George Chitwood's face, just to the left of his nose, from point-blank range, and the mountaineer fell dead into the buggy.[173] As George Chitwood died, Oscar Chitwood got up and remounted his horse. Sid Houpt turned and fired once at Oscar, the bullet shattering Oscar's left elbow and disabling his arm as he rode away.[174]

As Oscar Chitwood pushed his horse at breakneck speed away from the courthouse, Sid Houpt had options. He could have rushed to his wounded brother and tried to save his life. He might have gathered reinforcements and formed a posse to pursue Chitwood. Both were perfectly reasonable options. However, without any apparent hesitation, Sid Houpt ran to the buggy tied up near the courthouse, dumped George Chitwood's dead body to the ground and took off alone in hot pursuit of Oscar Chitwood.[175]

Sid Houpt's gun "had but a few loads left." He had been unarmed just a few minutes before and was using a borrowed revolver that probably held six rounds. There is no indication that Houpt had any more ammunition than what the gun contained. Sid Houpt had fired at least three shots—with his first round, he hit Oscar Chitwood's saddle; he killed George Chitwood with another bullet; and he maimed Oscar Chitwood with one more.[176] Studies of police shootings conducted from 1863 to 1992 show members of law enforcement rarely hit their targets more than 30 percent of the time.[177] Assuming Houpt enjoyed 100 percent accuracy, which would be extraordinary in the adrenaline rush of an impromptu gunfight, he had no more than three bullets left to confront a dangerous, armed man, who was fleeing in the direction of the Chitwood family farm, where he was likely to find reinforcements. Sid Houpt may have suffered from many faults, but he was not a coward.

News of the shootout spread quickly, and men in the community rushed to help Sid Houpt. Courthouse clerks Robert Mooney and Alf Whittington spread news of the shootout by word of mouth, telephone and telegraph.

When Whit Stearns of Stearns Hardware learned that Sid Houpt had taken off in hot pursuit of a dangerous criminal with an almost empty pistol, he took two Winchester rifles, two Colt pistols and pile of ammunition off the shelf, loaded it all into an automobile and sent a clerk to deliver the weapons and help Houpt. Deputy Doc Walz, who typically worked the night shift, joined Sid Houpt's pursuit. Within an hour after the shootout ended, posses of heavily armed men swarmed the county, looking for Oscar Chitwood. Constable DeVail and John Davis rushed to the Chitwood family farm and found that the outlaws had prepared for trouble by prepositioning five large-caliber rifles in defensive positions on the property.[178]

Oscar Chitwood moved west toward his mother's home between the communities of Bear and Mountain Pine. He paused and found a hiding spot near the bridge over Bull Bayou where he could see the road while remaining concealed. In the confusion, Oscar had not realized that his brother was dead, and he waited near Bull Bayou in hopes that his brother would find him there. While he waited, he tore his shirt and tried to craft it into a crude sling for his disabled left arm. He watched two separate armed posses cross the bridge just a short distance away.[179]

About midnight, Oscar gave up on his brother and crossed the stream below the bridge. He arrived at his mother's house early the next morning and was disappointed to find that his mother was not home. Oscar Chitwood did not know it, but his mother and aunt were in Hot Springs, identifying the dead body of George Chitwood at McCafferty's morgue. A witness reported that neither woman displayed any emotion as they identified George's body, suggesting that "they are poor people, acquainted with hard situations, and with hard experiences." While at his mother's house, Oscar Chitwood exchanged his worn-out horse for a fresh one and gathered provisions, then went into hiding in the woods of western Garland County. Later that day, he bumped into a friend, who informed him that George Chitwood was dead, Jake Houpt was badly wounded and posses were determined to find Oscar.[180]

While some residents took up arms and fanned out in search of Oscar Chitwood, other townsfolk focused on helping the wounded sheriff. Men carried Jake Houpt to his home on Moore Street, about a mile east of the courthouse, where Dr. Randolph treated the wounded lawman.[181] Hundreds of people visited the Houpt home to express their sympathy and offer to help the family. Leading men in Hot Springs offered a reward of $1,250 to anyone who could successfully bring Oscar Chitwood to justice.[182] The reward was a huge sum in an era when most skilled workers in Arkansas

Gravestone of George and Martha Chitwood. *Courtesy of Christopher Thrasher.*

Arkansas Gazette.

NINETY-FIRST YEAR. LITTLE ROCK, THURSDAY, AUGUST 18, 1910. PRICE FIVE CENTS PER COPY

SHERMAN WILL NOT BOW TO ROOSEVELT

Vice President Declares He Will Not Withdraw in Colonel's Favor and Deprecates Fight Reports.

A CONFERENCE OVER REBUKE

Taft to Compose Campaign Letter—Cannon's Attitude Cause of General Lamentation.

ALABAMA FARMERS OPPOSE SULLY PLAN

National President Barrett Says It Means Loss of Producers' Rights—General Opposition Predicted.

CHICAGOAN CROSSES CHANNEL WITH MAN

Unknown Architect, on Sixth Flight, Flies From Calais to Tilmanstone, Carrying a Passenger.

FEAT IN TEETH OF A GALE

GAYNOR PASSES BEST DAY SINCE INJURED

Despite Most Hopeful Bulletins, Disquieting Rumors Spread Throughout New York, Meeting Denial.

TAP-LINES WILL OPEN FIGHT HERE

Application for Injunction Against the Rock Island Railway Company Will Be Filed Today.

LUMBER ROAD IS PLAINTIFF

Malvern and Freeo Valley Road Charges that Trunk Line Has Violated Its Contract.

FRAUD IN TICKET SELLING

Sheriff Houpt Mortally Wounded; Outlaw Killed In Hot Springs Street

Armed Posses Search Mountains for Another Desperado Who Probably Will Never Be Captured Alive—Tragedy in Shadow of Courthouse.

THINK FUGITIVE WOUNDED

Hot Springs, 2:30 A. M., Aug. 18.—Dr. J. W. Smith, one of the four physicians who are in attendance on Sheriff Jake Houpt, just left the patient's bedside and said that the chances were very much against Sheriff Houpt's recovery.

"I should say that he had one chance in ten," said Dr. Smith. "His temperature and pulse are rising, both of which are bad symptoms."

Attending physicians state that Sheriff Houpt exhibited remarkable fortitude. He described to them the shooting in detail and, although fully appreciating the seriousness of his condition, declared that he would recover. This afternoon he sent for Circuit Clerk Alf Whittington and gave minute directions concerning the affairs of his office, in case he should die.

Deputy Sheriff Sid Houpt and his party returned at 1:30 o'clock this morning for fresh horses, after an unsuccessful quest for the fugitive. He says he found trace of blood along the route taken by the outlaw and he is confident that Oscar Chitwood is seriously wounded. He believes that Chitwood is hiding somewhere in the Ragweed Valley district and that his capture is only a question of a short time. Houpt and his men started out again immediately.

Arkansas Gazette front page describing the shootout between the Chitwoods and the Houpts. *Courtesy of* Arkansas Gazette.

made less than 50¢ per hour.[183] Initially, Jake Houpt feared that he had only a short time to live, but after Dr. Randolph stopped the bleeding and made him comfortable, the sheriff began to believe that he might survive. By the end of the evening, he felt well enough to summon county clerks to his bedside, where he provided instructions on business and legal matters.[184] A local journalist suggested that the sheriff was "fighting for his own life with that same grit and courage he showed when wounded in battle."[185]

After several days of hiding, a hungry, dirty and badly battered Oscar Chitwood decided to turn himself in on August 20, 1910. He approached Jim Coleman, a relative, and asked Coleman to surrender him to the authorities. Coleman and his neighbor John Bryant loaded the badly wounded fugitive into the back of Coleman's wagon and turned him over to Deputies Ben Murray and John Rutherford. The deputies took Chitwood to Dr. Shaw, who treated Chitwood's injuries. Dr. Shaw noted that, in addition to the gunshot to his arm, Chitwood was also suffering from various minor injuries, and he was still wearing the gun belt that was cut in two places by the lawmen's bullets that did not penetrate Chitwood's body. Chitwood admitted to fleeing from the courthouse but claimed, "I never fired a shot."[186]

In a society where lynching was common, members of law enforcement understood that they never enjoyed a monopoly on violence. They were forced to walk a fine line between protecting society from criminals and protecting prisoners in their custody from citizens who might take the law into their own hands at any moment. Rutherford and Murray feared that a lynch mob might rush the jail and murder Oscar Chitwood before he could have his day in court, so as soon as Dr. Shaw treated Chitwood's wounds, the two deputies loaded their prisoner into a car and drove him to the Arkansas State Penitentiary in Little Rock. The trip to Little Rock was unpleasant for both the deputies and the passenger. A heavy rain drenched all three men in the open car. The car skidded and bounced over the rough and slippery road as Ben Murray pushed the car to its maximum speed to escape the lynch mob they feared was following. A local journalist suggested that the deputies' haste was "a wise precaution," since "public sentiment is extremely high against Chitwood over the shooting."[187]

Oscar Chitwood was safe for the moment, but the wounded sheriff was not. Jake Houpt died of his wounds at 10:10 p.m. on Saturday, August 20, 1910, surrounded by doctors and family members who made his last moments as comfortable as possible. Houpt might have survived the gunshot itself, but the wound caused pneumonia, which was Houpt's official cause of death. The local newspaper praised Jake Houpt's "courageous struggle against

Jake Houpt's grave. *Courtesy of Christopher Thrasher.*

death" and proclaimed him "a martyr to the duties of his office." The departed sheriff left behind a widow, Fannie, and three children aged five and younger.[188] The funeral took place on August 21 in the family home on Moore Street. The Reverend Forney Hutchinson of the First Methodist Church officiated the service. After the funeral, a public procession led by members of Mason Lodge No. 62 took Jake Houpt's remains to the family plot at Ten Mile Cemetery in neighboring Saline County.[189] Leading citizens of Hot Springs held a series of meetings to eulogize the fallen sheriff, organize efforts to commemorate his memory and provide for his widow and orphans.[190]

Oscar Chitwood, from the *Arkansas Gazette*, August 21, 1910.

While the friends and family of Jake Houpt laid him to rest, Oscar Chitwood made his first official statement on August 20. From the state prison in Little Rock, Oscar Chitwood gave an extensive interview, in which he gave his side of the story. His injuries were still fresh, but prison doctors gave Chitwood "a great quantity of opiates" to help him deal with his pain. Chitwood sat up, but he did not leave his prison cot for his testimony. Despite the large doses of painkillers coursing through Chitwood's body, a reporter described him as "clean cut" with "steel gray eyes that never faltered." A newspaper photographer took Oscar Chitwood's photograph while he sat in his cot. It is the only known photograph of either Chitwood brother. In the poor-quality image, Oscar Chitwood sits up, bare chested and bandaged. His head rests against a pillow. The metal cot frame is barely visible. Chitwood's mouth and eyes are closed. The unnamed reporter who took Chitwood's statement suggested that Chitwood was honest, or at least earnest, writing that the prisoner told his story "in sincere tones."[191]

Oscar Chitwood categorically rejected all claims that he was a criminal. Disputing claims that he had been convicted of theft and spent time in a Texas prison, Chitwood claimed that he "had a clean record," had spent his time away from Arkansas working as a carpenter and could "prove" he had never been convicted of any crimes. Chitwood argued that "all of this has grown out of lying and gossiping tongues" that originated in "a family grudge which existed before I was born."[192]

Chitwood stated that when he heard the claims that he was a horse thief, he wrote Sheriff Houpt to protest the charge and offered to surrender himself if Houpt had a warrant. Chitwood explained that he initially tried to handle the matter in writing rather than by going in person to face the accusations he was a thief because "I didn't want to be mobbed." It is possible that Chitwood's claim was dishonest, that he did not fear getting "mobbed" and that he only made this claim in an effort to explain his failure to turn himself in. However, his claim is revealing, even if it was a lie. By explaining his behavior in terms of fears of mob justice, Chitwood revealed his belief that people would understand threats of vigilante justice and treat his concerns sympathetically. Chitwood might or might not have feared getting mobbed, but he clearly believed that his fears of lynch mobs would resonate with area residents and perhaps potential jurors. After writing the letter to Sheriff Houpt, Chitwood claimed that Houpt replied by informing both him and his mother, in writing, that there were no warrants for Oscar Chitwood's arrest.[193]

Oscar Chitwood claimed that he and his brother went to Jake Houpt's office on the morning of August 17 in response to Sid Houpt's request and were once again exonerated when Jake Houpt confirmed that he did not have an arrest warrant for either brother, and they chatted "for fully an hour" before the Chitwood brothers left the sheriff's office. The Chitwood brothers were in the process of mounting their horses when Sid Houpt came outside and asked both George and Oscar Chitwood to come back to Jake Houpt's office. Oscar Chitwood claimed that he and George agreed and went back inside, where they found that the sheriff's office was empty. They waited a short time until the Houpts rushed in and grabbed the Chitwoods, now claiming that they had a warrant for their arrest. Oscar Chitwood admitted that being grabbed "made me mad," so he pulled his pistol so he and his brother could escape. Perhaps pulling his pistol was Chitwood's worst crime, a singular mistake, or perhaps Chitwood's admission to pulling a gun when the Houpts "made me mad" revealed more than the wounded man realized. Consistent with the testimony of other witnesses, Oscar Chitwood reported that he and his brother were untying their horses when the Houpt brothers confronted them with drawn pistols. Oscar Chitwood claimed that the Houpts opened fire without warning.

A reporter described Oscar Chitwood as appearing "sincere" as he expressed regret for the incident and worried that "this business will kill my mother and sister." Chitwood admitted to fleeing the courthouse on August 17 to avoid arrest but argued, "I am not a desperado," and insisted, "I did not fire a single shot during the affair." He seemed to suggest that his dead brother was solely responsible for the bullets that flew toward the Houpts, claiming that, while he was focused entirely on escaping, he "did not know what George did." When Chitwood mentioned events before the day of the shootout, he reportedly said, "I was not a bad man."[194] While the difference between present and past tense in the record might be nothing more than the clumsy grammar of a man with painkillers coursing through his body or the transcription error of a reporter, it is also possible that Chitwood was admitting that the day of the shootout had changed him, that he entered the courthouse "not a bad man" but became something different that day.

Oscar Chitwood repeatedly demanded to know about the bullet that killed Jake Houpt. He claimed that while he and his brother both carried .38 revolvers, George's revolver fired .38 regular cartridges, and Oscar's revolver fired far more potent .38 special cartridges. Oscar Chitwood claimed that forensic evidence would prove that he did not kill Jake Houpt, but the coroner refused to reveal the details of Jake Houpt's death.[195] The coroner did examine Jake Houpt's body and even called witnesses, but the coroner's records appear to be missing from the county archives. This could be evidence of a coverup. However, it is also possible that the records were misfiled or destroyed in the 1913 fire that gutted the courthouse and destroyed many county records. Many of the county records from before 1913 that do survive bear unmistakable scorch marks.

Multiple witnesses disputed Oscar Chitwood's claim that he did not fire his gun and reported "he was firing constantly" during the incident.[196] While witnesses disputed his claims of total innocence, they all seemed to concede that Oscar Chitwood was not a murderer. All available witnesses quoted in the local newspapers stated that they saw George shoot Jake Houpt at close range, and all of them believed that George's bullet killed Jake Houpt, since Houpt fell almost as soon as he was hit. Meanwhile, those same witnesses noted that Oscar was some distance away, struggling to get out from under his fallen horse.[197] W.B. Steed, a friend of Sid Houpt who watched the gunfight from a few feet away, stated that Oscar Chitwood fired just one round, and the shot was fired into the air at the start of the shootout, in a clear attempt to scare away the lawmen without hurting them.[198] Chitwood's friends in the county believed that he had not intended to hurt anyone because he was known as an excellent marksman, and "if he had fired he would not have wasted any bullets."[199]

Although nobody testified that Oscar Chitwood murdered Jake Houpt, the court held Chitwood without bond.[200] The prosecution pointed out

Printed and for Sale by Claude Mann, Malvern, Arkansas.

INDICTMENT.

STATE OF ARKANSAS, against Oscar Chitwood.

In the Garland Co. Circuit Court, INDICTMENT.

The Grand Jury of Garland County, in the name and by the authority of the State of Arkansas, accuse Oscar Chitwood of the crime of Assault to kill and murder committed as follows, to-wit: The said Oscar Chitwood in the County and State aforesaid, on the day of August, A. D. 1910,

unlawfully ,feloniously,and with malice aforethought,wilfully and deliberately did make an assault upon one,Sid Houpt,with a deadly weapon,to-wit: a gun,by then and there shooting at him,the said Sid Houpt,with the said gun,loaded with gun powder and leaden balls, and then and there held in the hands of him,the said Oscar Chitwood, with the intent then and there to kill and murder him,the said Sid Houpt,

against the peace and dignity of the State of Arkansas.

C. T. Cotham
Special Prosecuting Attorney.

Indictment of Oscar Chitwood. *Courtesy of Garland County Courthouse.*

that, even before the shootout, Oscar Chitwood was a wanted criminal. They also argued that, even if the witnesses were correct, and Oscar Chitwood did not murder Jake Houpt, the man freely admitted that he tried to avoid arrest. Perhaps most importantly, prosecutors argued that, by firing the first shot, even though it was fired into the air, Oscar Chitwood initiated a lethal confrontation and therefore deserved to pay the penalty for Jake Houpt's death.[201]

Several days after reporters visited Oscar Chitwood to get his side of the story, L.A. Carr and F.L.F. Devinney visited Chitwood to confront him about stealing a horse. Devinney claimed that a few days before the August 17 shootout, the Chitwood brothers handed over a horse as part of a trade. Carr claimed that the horse was his property and that somebody had stolen it. Oscar Chitwood admitted that the horse he traded to Devinney was stolen, but he claimed that he got it in an honest trade from a man named Norman who lived in Ragweed Valley.[202] Chitwood maintained that he did not steal the horse, and his admission does not prove that he was a horse thief, but the combination of multiple accusations with Chitwood's admission that he was in possession of stolen property does cast doubts on his claims of total innocence.

While the Garland County court held Chitwood without bond, Governor George Washington Donaghey appointed Sid Houpt to the now-vacant post of Garland County sheriff. Sid Houpt was an obvious choice to fill the vacancy. He was an experienced lawman who served as his brother's chief deputy and right-hand man. A delegation of leading citizens from Garland County publicly supported Houpt's appointment and presented the governor with a petition requesting Sid Houpt's appointment signed by 1,500 citizens of Hot Springs. No other candidate formally applied for the job, and nobody publicly announced any opposition to Sid Houpt's candidacy.[203] While these were important factors in the governor's decision to promote Sid Houpt, "the governor was further influenced by the plucky fight put up by Sid Houpt after his brother had been shot down, when the deputy officer, after sending a bullet through George Chitwood, followed hard on the trail of Oscar Chitwood."[204]

By approaching the Chitwoods unarmed and by initially attempting to arrest them without resorting to violence, Sid Houpt indicated that he was a man of the praying South rooted in the pacifistic morality of the Second Great Awakening, as described by Ted Ownby. By springing into action when threatened and sending bullets crashing into each of the Chitwood brothers in turn, Sid Houpt demonstrated that he was also more than just a man of peace. As Grady McWhiney has argued, "The darkest side of the southerner is his quarrelsomeness, and recklessness of human life."[205] By shooting two dangerous outlaws, Sid Houpt demonstrated that he was willing to kill if needed and embodied the dark southern virtue of recklessness with the lives of others. Perhaps more importantly, by tearing off in hot pursuit of a dangerous fugitive alone, with a nearly empty pistol, Sid Houpt proved that he was willing to risk his life to bring a dangerous outlaw to justice, demonstrating that he was reckless with his own life as well as with the lives of others. The August 17 encounter with the Chitwoods lasted only a few minutes, but in those few minutes, Sid Houpt proved that he could balance the pacifistic nonviolence of the praying South with the "recklessness of human life" the governor clearly valued in lawmen forced to confront dangerous criminals. Sid Houpt's actions on August 17 impressed the governor, cemented his support among leading men of Hot Springs and made him Garland County's next sheriff.[206]

While Sid Houpt earned praise from city and state leaders, Deputies Ben Murray and John Rutherford enraged many of the same people when they tried to claim the reward for capturing Oscar Chitwood. Under Arkansas law, members of law enforcement were not entitled to rewards for actions they performed as part of their job duties. When the public discovered that the Murray and Rutherford, paid deputies, were illegally trying to collect the reward, local citizens condemned them as "greedy."[207] The deputies then changed their story, claiming that they only requested the reward so that they could hand it over to Jake Houpt's widow. At the same time, Jim Coleman and John Bryant, the two farmers who helped Oscar Chitwood turn himself in, also claimed the reward. Ultimately, Judge Curl and Judge Evans ruled that nobody deserved the reward, since Chitwood had turned himself in.[208] In response, Jim Coleman and John Bryant sued deputies Ben Murray and John Rutherford for $12,000, arguing that they made false statements in public and in legal proceedings that deprived them of the reward and damaged their standing in the community.[209] It does not appear that the lawsuit went anywhere, but the local press covered the story, which may have further diminished Murray and Rutherford in the eyes of the local community and left them looking for an opportunity to redeem themselves.

At the state penitentiary in Little Rock, Oscar Chitwood received medical treatment and began to recover from his wounds.[210] James L. Graham, of Hot Springs, became Chitwood's lawyer and met with him to prepare a defense. Graham publicly complained that prison guards were mistreating Chitwood, primarily by denying him access to the outdoor recreation yard despite the fact that Chitwood's doctor recommended time outdoors as part of his physical therapy and that almost all prisoners, including those awaiting execution, were given that privilege.[211] It is unclear if the guards prevented Chitwood from exercising outdoors in an effort to punish him, as Graham suggested, or because they thought it would keep him safe. Deputies originally brought Chitwood to Little Rock to protect him from a lynch mob. Prison guards might have been concerned that it would be hard to protect Chitwood in an open prison yard. Alternately, the guards might have worried that Chitwood would try to escape. They reported that when

Oscar Chitwood arrived at the prison, they searched him, and "seven saws were discovered sewed in the upper part of his vest."[212]

On November 9, 1910, the grand jury indicted Oscar Chitwood on charges of murdering Jake Houpt, being an accessory before the fact to the murder and assault with intent to kill Sid Houpt.[213] On November 15, newly appointed sheriff Sid Houpt visited Oscar Chitwood in the state penitentiary to inform him personally about the grand jury's indictment. Houpt could have informed Chitwood of the indictment by mail, telegraph or telephone or through Chitwood's attorney, but for some reason, Houpt delivered the news personally. Sadly, no transcript of the conversation between the two men—who last saw each other during the gunfight that left both men grieving for a dead brother—survives. Available accounts only state that Chitwood was "little moved by the reading of the indictments."[214]

On December 7, 1910, Garland County deputy John Rutherford came to the state prison in Little Rock, chained Oscar Chitwood to his body and brought the prisoner back to Hot Springs for trial.[215] Chitwood was scheduled for trial in Garland County, but there was a preliminary conflict over the location of the proceedings. Chitwood's lawyer, James L. Graham, petitioned the court for a change of venue. He argued that Chitwood would not get a fair trial in Hot Springs, where nearly every member of the community believed that Chitwood was guilty and where the Houpt family wielded tremendous influence. The prosecutor contested Graham's petition, pointing out that juries must be drawn from the community where the crime took place.[216] After careful deliberation, Judge Evans granted the defense's motion for a change of venue. The trial would take place in Benton, located between Hot Springs and Little Rock, and was tentatively scheduled for March 1911.[217]

On the morning of December 26, 1910, the front page of the *Sentinel-Record* newspaper read: "Oscar Chitwood Shot and Killed by Men."[218] According to Deputy John Rutherford, at one forty-five that morning, he entered the county jail with plans to remove Chitwood and escort him to the city jail, near the railroad tracks, for a train trip to the state penitentiary in Little Rock, where he would await trial in Benton.[219] According to Rutherford's testimony, Chitwood's right arm was through his coat sleeve, and his coat's left sleeve was draped over his still-injured left arm. Rutherford claimed that he handcuffed both of Chitwood's wrists together but did not shackle Chitwood to himself as he had done when he brought Chitwood back to Hot Springs.[220] Rutherford stated that at about two o'clock, he exited the courthouse through the door on the east side of the building with Chitwood.[221]

Rutherford further claimed that, as he and Chitwood entered a small enclosure, which concealed the gallows where Harry Poe had been executed on September 2, 1910, a group of armed, masked men confronted Rutherford and told him that they would kill him unless he stood aside. Rutherford stated that he stood by helplessly, afraid, as he watched the men gun down Chitwood at point-blank range and then disappear into the darkness a moment later.[222] Most residents sleeping in nearby homes thought little of the gunshots, assuming they were "Christmas guns" fired in celebration rather than anger. As soon as the shooting ended, Rutherford notified other deputies and the city police of the incident.[223] Ben Murray was the only other deputy listed as on duty at the courthouse that night.[224] Sheriff Sid Houpt was away from Hot Springs with his wife and son, visiting his sister in Rosebud, Texas.[225]

Initially, newspapers uncritically repeated John Rutherford's claims that masked men lynched Oscar Chitwood. The Hot Springs *Sentinel-Record* quoted Rutherford's account that "masked men shot Chitwood to death."[226] The *Arkansas Democrat*'s front page for December 26 stated, "Chitwood Riddled with Bullets by Mob" and reported Rutherford's account with little apparent skepticism.[227] The *Vicksburg Evening Post* in Mississippi condemned Oscar Chitwood as "a white murderer" who was "lynched by mob."[228] The *Chattanooga News* of Tennessee stated that "a furious band of twenty five men" overpowered Rutherford and "lynched" Chitwood because he murdered Sheriff Houpt.[229] The *Butte Daily Post* in Montana seemed to approve of Chitwood's death, which it described as an example of a lynch mob "administering some lead pellets" to a murderer.[230] The *Tacoma Times* in faraway Washington State repeated Rutherford's story that mysterious "masked men" murdered Chitwood.[231] Even today, lists of lynching victims often include Chitwood's name. Oscar Chitwood was lynched. There was no doubt whatever about that.

CHAPTER 4

LYNCHING, RACE AND LAWMEN

O, what may man within him hide,
Though angel on the outward side!
How may likeness made in crimes,
Making practise on the times,
To draw with idle spiders' strings
Most ponderous and substantial things!

—*William Shakespeare,* Measure for Measure

Oscar Chitwood may not have actually been lynched, but he was exactly the type of white man who could have found himself at the end of a rope.

But before we get to him, we should unpack that term—*lynching*—just a bit, for it has meant different things to different people over the course of American history. Those studying the American West have typically regarded lynching as the "rough justice" of the frontier directed at obvious criminals and outlaws usually as white as the mobs who lynched them, in a time and place where the instruments of "proper" justice were rather lacking. For these scholars, the lynching of an African American man (or a Latino, Asian or Native) constituted an aberration of normal practices. Meanwhile, those studying the American South have emphasized how lynching primarily constituted a means of terrorizing and subjugating African Americans. In this schema, white lynching victims were the definite exception to the deadly rule.

Some scholars have attempted to combine these various perspectives to argue that lynching underwent a certain kind of "evolution" over the centuries, a view outlined eloquently by Ashraf H.A. Rushdy:

> *In the first stage, frontier societies lynch those accused of crimes against property in the early days of settlement, while the territory still lacks legal and judicial apparatus. In the second stages, primarily homicide or other especially heinous crimes are punished by lynching, sometimes in the absence of the legal apparatus, often despite its presence. In the third stage, vigilante violence becomes a tool for capitalists to dominate particular fields.... Finally, in the last stage, lynching becomes a weapon of terrorism used to control the mobility of particular groups (defined along ethnic, racial, or class lines).*[232]

Such a schema is elegant and offers some hope of reconciling differing views as to the "real story" of American lynching, but unfortunately, its own center does not hold. Ken Gonzales-Day's study of lynching in California, to give one example, uncovered how extensively racialized the practice of "mob justice" was in this frontier state, targeting primarily those of Hispanic origin.[233] In addition, significant work in the history of the lynching of slaves has begun to undermine the story of a "pre-racial" lynching of the antebellum era that was eventually supplanted by a post–Civil War form of violence that almost exclusively targeted African Americans. In Arkansas, four white men were lynched between 1836, the year of statehood, and 1861. By contrast, as the figures now stand, one free Black man and sixteen enslaved men were lynched; there is even one source testifying to the lynching of an African American boy and a Native American man during this time.[234]

Another attempt to square the circle and present a unified perspective of lynching that can cover both white and nonwhite victims, without relying too much on analyzing geographical divisions or chronological evolution, comes from historian Brent M.S. Campney, who suggests "historians might investigate white-on-white lynchings from an explicitly racialized perspective—evaluating the ways that whites regulated fellow whites in relation to each other and to people of color, and questioning the motives of the mobs targeting whites as critically as those targeting people of color."[235] Drawing from the contributions made to the field of "whiteness studies" by the likes of David R. Roediger, Toni Morrison and Ruth Frankenberg, Campney proposes the following:

> *In the case of white-on-Black lynching, whites enforced their domination over people of color; in the case of white-on-white lynching, particular white people sought to enforce their domination over other people* within that race. *When more prosperous whites lynched poorer whites, for example, they were punishing those whites who failed to achieve the economic wherewithal synonymous with middle-class whiteness, marking them as trash and reinforcing the notion that whiteness was the antithesis of poverty and the key to privilege and power. In addition to these intra-racial class dynamics, whites revealed through white-on-white lynchings important insights into intra-racial ethnic, religious, gender, and sexual relations. Because white-on-white oppression occurred within a particular* racial *group, scholars should regard it as* racial—no more or less so than violence involving whites and Blacks. *White-on-white lynching, in other words, should illuminate class, ethnic, religious, gender, and sexual relations* among *whites in the same ways that white-on-Black mob violence illuminates social relations* between *whites and Blacks.*[236]

There are certainly differences of class and culture to be considered when looking at white victims of lynching, and the Chitwood murder speaks to this, given that the two brothers hailed from the rural, more hardscrabble part of the county—almost a different world compared to the cosmopolitan environment of Hot Springs—with their own personal economy based on sources outside the respectable confines of law and order. Oscar Chitwood would certainly have been regarded as "trash" by local elites.

Our point here is not to make a definitive statement about the nature of lynching in Arkansas specifically or the United States in general—it is simply to demonstrate that Oscar Chitwood was the sort of person who might have been targeted by a lynch mob in the very place and at the very time he was murdered, to demonstrate that those very early claims of mob justice were, in fact, credible to the population at large. We can see this by briefly surveying other cases of white-on-white lynching in Arkansas.

First, let us consider the initial crime with which the Chitwood brothers were charged—namely, horse theft. A number of white men were lynched for this very crime alone in the 1870s. The first was a man known only as McDonald, who was, according to a short article in the *Arkansas Gazette*, fatally shot on December 25, 1870, by a group of vigilantes from Springfield, Missouri, who had pursued suspected horse thieves into Marion County, Arkansas; another Arkansan, a man named Otterbury, was also shot but apparently survived his wounds.[237] A

Mississippi County farmer named Elias Holt was the next man killed in connection to horse thievery. In this case, a young man named Jones had been arrested and charged with horse stealing; he asserted that Holt had induced him to steal the horse and had plans to nab another, meet up with Jones in Jacksonport and run down to Texas to sell the beasts. Despite this statement coming from "a mere lad, who, in all probability, thought he might thereby mitigate his offense," Holt was warned to depart "by a band of disguised men." He proclaimed his innocence and stayed, only to be shot down on January 25, 1872.[238]

State vigilantes, however, were just warming up. On August 6, 1874, a mob broke into the jail in Sarber County (present-day Logan County) and took three prisoners away from town to hang them from the same tree. These three young men were William Harris, his brother Randolph and his brother-in-law Robert Skidmore, who reportedly constituted a gang that had terrorized the area for many years with murder and theft. The crime that saw them lynched, however, was the theft of several horses from Sarber County residents, after which they were tracked north to Washington County but could not be arrested. Harris discreetly returned to his parents' farm in Franklin County, only to be discovered there and arrested, along with Randolph Harris and Robert Skidmore. The mob that lynched these three men was described as between forty and one hundred men strong. The *Arkansas Gazette* stated that William Harris "preyed upon the community generally," engaging in a variety of crimes, but added, "Horse stealing and highway robbery was his vocation, and he applied it with energy."[239] A similar event took place in Polk County in southwestern Arkansas some three years later with the hanging of "an old man named Lebow" who had likewise terrorized his neighbors. As the *Fort Smith Independent* reported, in an article reprinted widely, "Many travelers have lost their horses, and many their lives, by the hands of Lebow, who has been employing his time for years in murder and highway robbery."[240]

In a replay of the 1870 lynching in Marion County, in October 1878, vigilantes from Missouri again pursued two ostensible horse thieves into Arkansas, this time into Carroll County, where the posse hanged both men from a tree.[241] The next man killed in connection with horse thievery was Elias Hensen, described by one newspaper as a "rather unsavory character in this neighborhood" who "was accused of various thefts, horse-stealing among them." However, after his arrest, he turned state's evidence against an accomplice and was ordered to present further evidence against other members of the local outlaw gang at the next term of court in Clay County.

A group of armed men showed up at the house where he was staying in eastern Randolph County on the night of March 12, 1879, and shot him to death, apparently to silence him forever.[242] Closing out the decade was the lynching of one William Yancey in Bradley County in May 1879. Yancey had been arrested in neighboring Calhoun County and charged with stealing horses and was apparently being transported to another jail when a posse intercepted those moving Yancey, took their prisoner and hanged him in the Lagle Creek bottoms.[243]

"Much American violence has been devoted to preserving the status quo," writes historian Richard Maxwell Brown. "The typical frontier vigilante movement was socially conservative. It was dedicated to the defense of traditional structure and values of the local community against the threatening presence of the criminal and the disorderly."[244] In addition, Brown notes, vigilante movements were typically "led by the element of the local community with the greatest stake in the status quo upheld by vigilantism: the elite group of leading businessmen, planters, and professionals."[245] And many of the men who became targets of vigilantes had committed crimes beyond the theft of horses, crimes such as murder and highway robbery, that certainly speak to a frontier conception of lynching as carried out by a community of upright people against those who constitute a "threatening presence." However, horse theft in particular constituted one of those touchstone crimes that precipitated the lynching of white men.

Indeed, vigilance groups formed around efforts to prevent and punish the theft of horses, the most notable of which was the Anti-Horse Thief Association (AHTA), which was founded in 1854 in Missouri and soon spread to multiple states. The organization operated like a fraternal lodge, with passwords and initiation ceremonies and standards of moral behavior for members, and its members sought to augment law enforcement rather than act as a vigilante substitute. In Arkansas, the AHTA was preceded by the Independent Order of the Knights of the Horse, founded in Crawford County in 1876. The AHTA did not appear in Arkansas until 1902, when regional leaders and those who headed up the Knights of the Horse met and endorsed a merger of their two groups; the state was granted its own charter in 1906 and held its first convention the following year.[246] The 1915 AHTA state division meeting in Fayetteville, which was also the national organization's annual meeting, hosted 125 delegates from across the state, with 75 more coming from around the country.[247] The organization started to fizzle out in the 1920s due largely to two factors: (1) the rise of more "exciting" social groups such as the renewed Ku Klux Klan and (2) the decreasing importance of horses in people's lives and economies. However, as Lynn Strawberry, author of a master's thesis on the AHTA in western Arkansas, writes:

> *When the Anti-Horse Thief Association was formed, horse stealing was a serious offence. Horses were a necessity of frontier life. They were needed for clearing forests, plowing ground and hauling freight as well as personal transportation. Horse thieves would be miles away before the sheriff could be notified. In reality, the only hope one had of retrieving stolen livestock was to go after the thief. If some neighbors went along, so much the better.*[248]

The theft of horses had motivated outright mob violence in the past, as well as the creation of a national organization that was arguably at the height of its power in the state by the time Oscar Chitwood and his brother were accused of horse stealing. But theft was not the crime for which he was killed—it was the murder of a lawman. And here, too, there is plenty of precedent when it comes to the lynching of whites in Arkansas.

For example, on May 17, 1892, a white man named Charles Stewart was lynched in Perryville for killing a deputy. He had been arrested, according to the *Arkansas Gazette*, "for attempted outrage on the 11-year-old daughter of J. W. Guin, and the subsequent stealing of a mule in March," and although such crimes alone had seen other men lynched, no Perryville residents reportedly threatened his life during the two months he was jailed. Stewart was shackled to the wall, the jail being insecure, and a deputy named Tom Holmes slept in the same room. On May 16, Stewart attacked and killed the deputy but was unable to escape, the door having been locked from the outside. The following morning, according to reports, Stewart "raised the alarm and claimed that Holmes had been murdered and thrown in his cell." This assertion, however, was not believed: "The enraged citizens took Stewart out to a convenient tree and hanged him."[249] A similar fate awaited George Shivery in Pocahontas after having allegedly shot and killed a city marshal named John Norris, who was described in newspaper accounts as "a Knight of Pythias, married, and [having] left four children." Shivery was subsequently arrested and indicted, but on the night of March 22–23, 1901, just two days after the murder, a mob described as numbering four to five hundred broke into the jail, despite the pleas of the local sheriff to let the criminal justice system deal with Shivery, and took their victim to a county bridge, from which they hanged him.[250]

Norris was apparently highly esteemed not only as a marshal but as a citizen, given his membership in a local fraternal organization, and the murder of such a man could easily ignite a lynch mob, as George Shivery discovered, and as Zallie Cadle would discover just two years later. Cadle and a friend named Charlie Simmons rolled into the community of Brinkley on the morning of November 7, 1903, and began drinking. By the time local marshal J.C. Cox encountered them near evening, they were "in a boisterous humor and ready for trouble." Cox tried to persuade them to quit the scene and head home, and when they refused, he threatened arrest. During the fight that followed, Cadle struck Cox across the neck with his knife, slashing the jugular vein. Cadle and Simmons were soon arrested, and Cox died later that night. After midnight, a mob consisting of "all the best citizens of the town" entered the jail without trouble and, after an apparent scuffle with Cadle, hanged the murderer from a nearby telegraph pole. A report in the *Arkansas Democrat* described Cox, his victim, as "a man of irreproachable character and a splendid officer. He was everybody's friend."[251]

For his part, Andy Crum did not actually kill Mississippi County sheriff Sam Mauldin on July 31, 1915. But he did run the "blind tiger" on what was called Island 37, where the sheriff was murdered. The Mississippi River has, throughout its history, shifted course, but after the states along which it runs were established, the legal principle of avulsion held that any land that was part of one state but that, due to the shifting course of the river, ended up attached to another remained the property of its original owner. One such shift in 1876 left a chunk of what had been Tennessee now attached to Arkansas. As Arkansas lawmen had no jurisdiction there, and Tennessee lawmen were not inclined to make the long trip across the bridge at Memphis and then up to Mississippi County to patrol the area, the place consequently became a refuge for criminals and home to numerous "blind tigers" that sold bootleg whiskey. One of these, operated by Andy Crum, was among those raided by Sheriff Mauldin that fateful July day. However, the sheriff was killed not by Crum but by a Black man who was in the establishment at the time.[252] The report on Mauldin's death described him as "one of the best sheriffs Mississippi county has ever had," and the *Osceola Times* even included a front-page memorial to him headlined "Our Martyr," which observed that "our citizens loved the man for his sterling worth, and for his earnest endeavors to enforce the laws," while interestingly describing the sheriff's murderer as "a negro fiend, the tool of white scoundrels, too cowardly for the deed themselves."[253] Crum was arrested and had engaged lawyers to argue that he should be tried in Tennessee, rather than in Arkansas, but on

August 12, a group of about a dozen men overpowered the jailor and shot Crum eight times, killing him. Interestingly, the report of his murder in the local newspaper described Crum as "the man who bought and paid for the weapons used in the murder of Sam D. Mauldin."[254]

So white men were lynched in Arkansas for much the same crimes as that of which Oscar Chitwood stood accused. In their 2015 study of the victims of lynching in the South, sociologists Amy Kate Bailey and Stewart E. Tolnay conclude that "while African American male victims were most likely to have been adolescents or young adult men, the average age for female and white victims was somewhat older," and "white men were most likely to have been accused of violent offenses or being of 'bad character.'"[255] This speaks to the Chitwood affair. He had a track record as a criminal and was regarded, still, as being an outlaw. He and his family lived in an unrespectable part of rural Garland County, and the fact that Chitwood had apparently changed family names over the course of his life would have said a lot to people of his era, for one who hailed from "good stock" would never be so cavalier with the inheritance of a family name. Although the newspaper record never makes use of the term, Chitwood exemplified a good deal of what falls under the label of "white trash" and was, as a consequence, exactly the sort of person who may have been killed by a mob.

But this is not the only thing that made interpreting what happened to him that night as a lynching, at least right off the bat, so plausible. We must also consider the role of the law—or, rather, of lawmen. The role of law enforcement in many events typically defined as lynchings does raise questions about the exact boundaries between the law and the mob, especially when a prisoner is taken from, or killed in the presence of, the police themselves, as Chitwood seemed to be. Sometimes, the police, at the very least, demurred from actually enforcing the law, not bothering to arrest people whom they witnessed carry out cold-blooded killings in the full light of day. And sometimes, the police facilitated mob actions or even actively cooperated with vigilantes.

To illustrate this, let us turn to an example that preceded the Chitwood murder by six years. The headline in the December 28, 1904 *Arkansas Gazette* relayed news of a horrible crime perpetrated on Christmas Day: "Mother and Child Shot to Death." The crime in question was the apparent rape and murder of Rachel Kincannon and her married daughter, Amelia Mauldin. The pair had left the town of Newport in northeastern Arkansas early Christmas morning to walk to the nearby community of Jacksonport, where Amelia's husband was lying sick. About an hour after the women crossed the White River via ferry, Amelia's body was discovered by "a respectable negro of Newport," who "hastened to town and sounded the alarm." Apparently, Amelia had been raped and shot twice; tracks indicated that the murderer or murderers had dragged her mother's body to the riverbank and thrown it in. Not knowing the identity of the perpetrators. Sheriff H.S. Simmons rousted and arrested a "camp of movers" but later released them, and newspapers also reported sightings of "a strange white man and a negro" who "had been seen walking several rods behind the two women a short time before the crime was committed."[256]

Within days, circumstantial evidence had implicated two men who were reported to have been following the women on Christmas morning, drunk.[257] The coroner's jury soon enough obtained the confession of Newton Allwhite, a nineteen-year-old white man, who told the investigators that he had acted at the order of his father, forty-three-year-old Louis Allwhite. The pair had reportedly raped mother and daughter and then carried the body of Rachel Kincannon to the river "and were returning to the scene of the crime to make similar disposal of the other body when some people were seen coming down the road," forcing them to flee.[258]

News of the confession sparked fears of mob violence in Newport, and Sheriff Simmons roped off the street across from the jail. However, at two o'clock in the afternoon, in the full light of day, a mob estimated at seven hundred people marched on the jail, overpowered the sheriff and guards and took possession of Louis Allwhite, leaving behind his son, Newton. Louis Allwhite was then marched two miles to a railroad trestle, near where the two women were murdered, and was hanged. The elderly James Kincannon, husband and father of the victims, "was carried to the scene of the hanging, which was also the scene of the tragedy, and looked with unconcealed pleasure upon the vengeance to [so?] speedily visited upon the destroyer of his home."[259]

A subsequent editorial in the *Gazette* described the original Christmas atrocity as "a double crime terrible enough to merit lynching if lynching is ever justifiable" but then went on to argue that this kind of mob violence is justifiable only "where justice will likely fail and where there is not the shadow of a doubt about the guilt of the accused":

> *As an action done on impulse has not the force and effect of an action done with deliberation, so an execution by a mob is not nearly such a great punishment to the victim and really not half so terrible a thing for the public to bear in its thoughts as spread with its tongue as for a sheriff*

> *coolly and deliberately to take a condemned prisoner from a cell[,] march him to the trap door of a gallows, bind him hand and foot, put the black cap over his face, knot the noose around his neck and then, amid the solemn silence of so gruesome an occasion, launch the lost wretch into an ignominious eternity.*[260]

Apparently, while the undisguised mob was marching down the public highway on New Year's Eve, "protest was made by prominent business men and lawyers in appeals to the crowd to await more convincing evidence of the man's guilt than given in the confession of his son, and under the circumstances then known, but all such attempts proved futile." However, a coroner's inquest into the murder of Louis Allwhite concluded that he "came to his death at the hands of an unknown mob."[261] The next day, the *Gazette* editorialized thusly: "Why should there be talk about the decline of humor? It isn't on decline at Newport."[262] Had these vigilantes come from outside the community, as was alleged in many cases of mob violence, no doubt that would have been indicated in reports of the event. Instead, we have every indication that officers of the law, as well as the prominent citizens of the community, could likely identify at least some of the members of the mob, but no effort was made to do so.

We can also glean from other events the possibility that lawmen actually assisted in the lynching of their prisoners through allowing themselves to be overpowered and/or through a convenient gullibility when it came to the tactics of the mob. Interestingly, there are accounts of both occurrences as they relate to a single event—the May 21, 1887 lynching of Andrew Springer in Powhatan in northeastern Arkansas. Springer, a white man, had allegedly raped a woman the previous week and was eventually tracked down and jailed. On the morning of May 21, according to an account in the *Arkansas Gazette*, a mob of some twenty-five men showed up at the jail, whereupon "the key's [*sic*] were demanded from the jailor, or force would be used." There is no indication in this report that force was actually used, and so we are led to assume that the threat alone sufficed to lead the jailor to disregard his duties and release his prisoner to this murderous mob. By contrast, the *Arkansas Democrat*'s account of the affair insisted that the mob acquired access to its target by means of subterfuge—namely, showing up at the house of the jailor and insisting that one of the men there, disguised somehow as a ruffian, needed to be detained. When the jail was unlocked, the mob held the jailor at gunpoint as they kidnapped Springer and whisked him away to be hanged. And here we have to ask just how gullible the jailor was determined to be, knowing that his high-profile prisoner might be the target of mob activity but nevertheless acquiescing when just such a mob appeared at his door in the early morning hours to demand that he open the jail.[263]

It seems, however, that lawmen were much more prone to assist vigilante mobs when the prisoner they had sworn to protect was African American. The lynching of Henry James in Little Rock highlights two different means by which policemen might facilitate a lynching. James was arrested on May 13, 1892, for having allegedly raped, three days before, the five-year-old daughter of his employer—exactly the sort of crime that would likely arouse mob violence. And the authorities knew it. The mayor ordered the transfer of James from the city to the county jail to protect municipal property from being damaged. But county authorities, knowing the situation, promptly absented themselves. Both the sheriff, Anderson Mills, and the chief deputy sheriff, Horace Booker, had mysteriously vanished by the time a reporter for the *Gazette* wound his way over to the jail to report on the unfolding story.[264] When leaders in law enforcement vanished like that, they were acknowledging that they readily expected violence to be inevitable and were disclaiming any responsibility for its prevention. And by leaving less experienced men in charge of situations that were rapidly spinning out of control, they made the aims of the mob that much easier to achieve.

But the lynching of Henry James highlights another way in which local authorities could facilitate the actions of the mob. Deputy Sheriff Jesse Heard, like the mayor before him, ordered the transfer of James to another facility, this time the state penitentiary there in Little Rock. When the mob showed up at the county jail and learned that James had been moved yet again, most of their number dispersed, but some traveled on to the next obvious possibility. There, Colonel S.M. Apperson, who was in charge of the place, ordered all the guards to retire to their own rooms for the night. He then went down to meet the mob, who had already attacked the driver of a hack whom they believed to have just transferred James, and acknowledged to the crowd that James was there and would be returned to county custody at eight in the morning. Apperson continued to refuse to give James over to the ever-growing mob, but in case they missed the hint embedded in his previous statement, he reminded them that James was due to be transferred back into county custody in the morning, "and then they could get him." However, the mob refused to wait and broke into the jail, and with all the guards in their own private quarters, the only resistance they experienced was that of locked doors.[265]

Perhaps the most egregious case of police assistance to the mob occurred leading up to the January 26, 1921 lynching of Henry Lowery in Mississippi

Garland County Sheriff's Fallen Officers Memorial. *Courtesy of Christopher Thrasher.*

County in northeastern Arkansas. Lowery had, on Christmas Day 1920, gone over to the home of his employer, plantation owner O.T. Craig, to confront him over a matter of payment. As Lowery was leaving the Craig house, he was fired on by one of Craig's sons, and in returning fire, he killed both O.T. Craig and his daughter Mary. Knowing what trouble awaited him, Lowery swiftly fled the area with help from members of a Black fraternal lodge and made his way to El Paso, Texas. He managed to remain hidden until late January 1921, when authorities intercepted a letter Lowery had written a friend. Lowery was arrested in El Paso, and Arkansas governor Thomas McRae managed to arrange for an expedited extradition with the proviso that the policemen sent to pick up Lowery would travel directly to Little Rock and immediately place their prisoner into the custody of the state penitentiary. However, as historian Karlos Hill writes, "Contrary to established protocol, Arkansas deputies blatantly violated Governor McRae's orders to take Lowery directly to Little Rock. Instead, they took a circuitous route that began in El Paso, then went to New Orleans, and then to a train station in Sardis, Mississippi," thus taking Lowery close to the scene of his original crime—and the home of the people who most wanted him dead. This route suggests, to Hill, "that authorities more than likely colluded with mob leaders, establishing the Sardis train station as the prearranged point for handing over Lowery to them." Indeed, members of the mob were already waiting in Sardis before the train arrived.[266] They took Lowery from the deputies without any resistance and transported him back to Nodena, Arkansas, where they slowly burned him to death. As historian Jeannie Whayne noted, one of the officers sent to retrieve Lowery was Jesse Greer, who only worked as a constable part time but had full-time employment with planter Lee Wilson, the brother-in-law of O.T. Craig.[267]

So, the history of lynching reveals that people like Oscar Chitwood were lynched for both general outlawry (especially horse stealing) and for the murder of policemen, especially when those officers were regarded as well-liked by the community at large. And we can also see how lawmen facilitated the murder of their charges without actually getting their hands bloody, sometimes even putting them in the direct line of the mob. Therefore, when the first stories of the lynching of Oscar Chitwood hit the newspapers, there was little to speak against this being yet another unfortunate (or convenient) case of vigilantism, on par with that which had been happening for decades—and would continue for a long time afterward. But soon enough, that story would fall apart, and Deputy John Rutherford would find himself on trial not for failing to defend Chitwood but for actively murdering him.

CHAPTER 5

"NO ONE HAS BEEN FOUND...WHO EVEN DIGNIFY IT BY REFERRING TO IT AS A LYNCHING"

Incidentally he reflected that the fellow dead there had been a noxious beast anyway; that men died every day in thousands; perhaps in hundreds of thousands—who could tell?—and that in the number, that one death could not possibly make any difference; couldn't have any importance, at least to a thinking creature.

—Joseph Conrad, "An Outpost of Progress"

Oscar Chitwood's death stunned people across the region, and some began doubting claims that Chitwood was lynched almost immediately. Chitwood's sister publicly accused the deputies of murdering her brother the day after the incident. Chitwood's lawyer, James L. Graham, accused the sheriff's department of "a deliberate conspiracy" to murder Chitwood.[268] J.P. Randolph, the coroner for Garland County, took the accusations seriously and empaneled a coroner's jury to investigate Chitwood's death in cooperation with prosecuting attorney J.B. Wood, a tough, reform-minded former judge known for crusading against illegal gambling and the officials, like the Houpts, who—he claimed—protected gamblers.

John Turner, a bartender and the first witness to see Chitwood's body, testified to the coroner's jury that when he arrived on the scene, Chitwood's coat was lying three feet away from his body. This contradicted Rutherford's claim that Chitwood was wearing a coat and that his wrists were handcuffed when he was shot.[269] When Rutherford was asked why Chitwood was not

Gravestone of Oscar Chitwood. *Courtesy of Christopher Thrasher.*

wearing his coat when Turner arrived, Rutherford suggested that it must have come off "during the scuffle."[270] Turner pointed out that Chitwood's wrists were still handcuffed when he found the body and wondered how the coat could have come off in a "scuffle" that left the handcuffs in place.[271]

C.H. Broughton testified to another odd bit of physical evidence at the murder scene. As covered in chapter 2, Harry Poe was executed on September 2, 1910, for supposedly attacking Lena Adams, a relative of Broughton. Shortly before Poe's execution, Broughton gave Sheriff Jake Houpt a rope and asked Houpt to hang Poe with it.[272] Houpt determined that Broughton's rope was too short and used another rope to hang Poe but kept Broughton's rope. Broughton claimed that he found the rope he gave Jake Houpt hanging over the scaffold used to hang Poe, near where Oscar Chitwood's body was found. Broughton wanted to know how a rope that was last seen in the hands of Jake Houpt came to rest on the scaffold just feet from Chitwood's body.[273]

Several witnesses living in homes near the courthouse the night of the murder independently claimed that they rushed to their windows when they heard gunshots and did not see a crowd of men during or after the shooting.[274] E.K. Sunderlind, staying in a boardinghouse across the street from the courthouse, claimed that he saw only a single person emerge from the gallows enclosure after the shooting ended.[275] Fred Olmstead, who lived across the street from the courthouse, testified that he woke up when he heard the shooting and was confident that no group of men left the courthouse grounds after the shooting.[276]

The coroner's jury briefly suspended their deliberations when Andrew Chitwood and Ruby Wright, brother and brother-in-law of the murdered man, appeared at the courthouse. Members of law enforcement searched the two men and found that each of them was carrying a loaded revolver. Authorities arrested both men on charges of carrying a concealed weapon, and the proceedings resumed.[277] It is unclear why the men illegally brought loaded guns to the courthouse, but the court released them on bond shortly after their arrests.[278]

Randolph called each of the eighteen prisoners held in the Garland County jail the night of Chitwood's murder to testify to the coroner's jury. Randolph realized that the prisoners, who were still in the custody of a sheriff's department accused of murdering Chitwood, were in a difficult spot. He cleared the room of all spectators when the prisoners testified and tried to keep their testimony secret; however, jurors soon shared prisoner testimony with journalists.[279] According to one juror, multiple prisoners testified that they heard Chitwood scream: "Oh, Mr. Houpt, for God's sake don't kill me. Let me stand trial." Since Jake Houpt was dead, and Sid Houpt was in Texas, this testimony suggested that deputy Reb Houpt might have been involved in Chitwood's murder, despite other testimony that Rutherford and Murray were the only deputies at the courthouse that night. Another prisoner testified that he watched Murray and Rutherford escort Chitwood to the courtyard, where they choked Chitwood with their hands as they announced their plan to string him up on the scaffold where Harry Poe had been executed. When Chitwood fought back, the deputies panicked, and one of them shot Chitwood.[280] If this account is accurate, it would explain why Broughton's rope was on the scaffold used to execute Poe.

On December 29, 1910, coroner Randolph ordered deputy sheriff Hardy Hinton to arrest Deputies John Rutherford and Ben Murray for the murder of Oscar Chitwood. As with Oscar Chitwood's arrest, authorities worried that a lynch mob might take the law into their own hands. Hinton held onto Rutherford's and Murray's arrest orders for several hours, only arresting the men when he could take them directly to a train leaving for Little Rock. Deputy Reb Houpt, the elder brother of the dead sheriff, helped Hinton escort the prisoners. As with Chitwood, whom Rutherford and Murray transported to Little Rock for safekeeping in August, Hinton and Reb Houpt took Rutherford and Murray to Little Rock because authorities in Hot Springs were worried about "the present excitement prevailing following the killing of Chitwood."[281]

On December 31, Sid Houpt returned to Hot Springs. After meeting with his lawyer, he stated that he first learned of Chitwood's death from a sheriff in Texas.[282] Shortly after speaking with said sheriff, Houpt reportedly received a letter from his niece, Bessie Tate, which stated that masked men had hanged Chitwood—Houpt learned that Chitwood had, in fact, been shot only after he and his family arrived in Hot Springs.[283] It is unclear why Tate claimed that Chitwood had been hanged, for the first newspaper accounts of the murder clearly state that Chitwood was shot. However, it does raise additional questions about why C.H. Broughton found his rope hanging over the scaffold a short distance from Chitwood's body. Sid Houpt stated that he had no firsthand information about Chitwood's murder but that he had the highest respect for both Murray and Rutherford. He expressed confidence that both men were innocent.[284]

Arkansans across the state condemned Chitwood's killers. Governor George Washington Donaghey declared himself "against lynching in every form" and called for the prosecution of any member of law enforcement who permitted a lynching. He condemned lynching on principle because it was "a crime of the highest order" that undermined the very foundations of government. Donaghey also loathed lynching because it convinced many outsiders that Arkansas was a lawless and dangerous place.[285] In response to claims by a St. Louis newspaper that the people of Arkansas endorsed lynching, the *Arkansas Democrat* argued that "the people of Hot Springs condemn that lynching as strongly as any people in any city."[286]

A writer for the *Arkansas Gazette* argued, shortly after the murder of Chitwood, that while lynching was "deplorable," it might be justified if several conditions were met. The author first argued that the crime must be so uniquely "heinous…that the passions of the people are aroused to the highest pitch." He suggested "the worst crimes against a woman" were particularly likely to result in a justifiable lynching. He next argued that a lynching could only be justified if it took place in the heat of the moment, "while the public mind is still hotly inflamed against" the criminal. Finally, a justifiable lynching must be conducted by "the men of a community." The idea that only the community, acting together, has the right to punish criminals is philosophically, although not legally, consistent with the Sixth

Amendment to the Constitution, which states that only a jury, composed of people living in the district where the crime was committed, has the right to declare someone guilty of a crime. The difference between a lynch mob made up of members of the community and those same people acting as a jury is an important distinction—but one that was often glossed over by those who felt lynching could be justified. After explaining how a lynching might be justified, the writer for the *Gazette* argued that Chitwood was not lynched, since he was killed long after the community's anger against him had cooled and not by the "men of a community" but by a small group of "cowards" who acted on their own without community support. The writer urged the authorities in Garland County "to bring to trial and punish the men who did the shameful deed."[287]

A writer for the *Sentinel-Record* publicly condemned Oscar Chitwood's murder thusly: "Never in the history of Hot Springs were the people of this city of one mind as they are in condemning the murder of Oscar Chitwood at the doors of the county jail Monday Morning. No one has been found since the particulars of the crime have become known who even dignify it by referring to it as a lynching."[288]

That article suggested that there was a certain dignity to lynching, to the men of the community coming together in response to an urgent threat and acting decisively to remove a danger to the most vulnerable members of their society. Despite the claims in the *Democrat* that "the people of Hot Springs condemn that lynching as strongly as any people in any city," documents from Hot Springs tell a very different story.[289] The writer in Hot Springs suggested that the people of that community condemned Chitwood's killers not because they lynched Chitwood, but because they did not lynch him.

Rutherford and Murray testified at the coroner's inquest on January 1, 1911. Both men acknowledged that it was odd for deputies to transfer a prisoner, without notifying higher authorities, in the middle of the night. However, they claimed that suspicious strangers were loitering around the courthouse earlier that day and that they were worried someone might be planning to break Oscar Chitwood out of jail. The deputies claimed that they believed that—by moving quickly, in the middle of the night, without alerting anyone else—they could safely transport Chitwood to the city jail and thwart the potential jailbreak.[290] While a potential jailbreak might seem like an odd conspiracy theory at first glance, several members of the Chitwood family had reputations as "desperate and law defying men."[291] The fact that two members of the Chitwood family illegally brought concealed firearms into the courthouse just days after Oscar Chitwood's death proves that several remaining members of the Chitwood family were potentially dangerous criminals.[292] Rutherford claimed that witnesses who testified to hearing Chitwood beg for his life were mistaken or lying and that they actually heard Rutherford begging the masked men not to murder him. [293]

On January 2, 1911, the coroner's jury concluded that "Oscar Chitwood came to his death at the hands of John Rutherford, Ben Murray, and others unknown to the jury." The "others unknown" who were responsible for Chitwood's death were never definitively named, but prosecutor Wood suggested that Reb Houpt was involved in the murder.[294] Reb Houpt remained free, but Rutherford and Murray were held without bond.[295] The two prisoners petitioned the court for bail, arguing that they had ties to the community and would not flee since they looked forward to the trial, which they argued would exonerate them.[296] On January 31, Judge Henry Evans denied Rutherford's and Murray's applications for bail and ordered Sid Houpt to hold both men in the county jail to await trial.[297] In spite of the court order, on February 15, Sid Houpt allowed Murray and Rutherford to leave the jail and live with their families. When Judge Evans learned that Rutherford and Murray were not confined to the county jail, he remanded both men to the Hot Springs city jail to be held without bail pending their upcoming trials.[298]

On April 15, 1911, the Garland County grand jury indicted both John Rutherford and Ben Murray for the first-degree murder of Oscar Chitwood.[299] Consistent with the findings of the coroner's jury, the grand jury found that Murray and Rutherford had conspired together with "unknown" others to murder Chitwood. Surviving grand jury records do not conclusively identify the "unknown" others, but prosecutor J.B. Wood suggested that Reb Houpt was involved.[300] The court renewed orders to hold both Murray and Rutherford in the Hot Springs city jail while they awaited trial.[301] J.B. Wood announced that he would continue to seek indictments against other people involved in the murder of Oscar Chitwood.[302]

On the same day the Garland County grand jury indicted Murray and Rutherford, it also handed down nineteen other indictments. The grand jury indicted Sid Houpt on two counts of "the crime of escape" because he failed to follow the court's orders to keep Ben Murray and John Rutherford confined in the county jail and instead allowed both men to travel freely and live at home with their families. While it was true that both men remained nearby and that neither man missed any required court appearances, prosecuting attorney J.B. Wood argued that, by allowing both men to leave the jail, contrary to court orders, Sid Houpt was technically guilty of helping

INDICTMENT.

STATE OF ARKANSAS,
Against
John Rutherford,

Garland Circuit Court
INDICTMENT.

The Grand Jury of Garland County, in the name and by the authority of the State of Arkansas, accuse John Rutherford of the crime of murder in the first degree committed as follows: The said John Rutherford in the County and State aforesaid, on the 26th day of Dec. A. D., 1910 and one Ben Murray and others to the Grand Jurors unknown did then and there feloniously ,willfully,deliberately and of their malice aforethought and with premeditation and deliber ation kill and murder one Oscar Chitwood by then and there willfully, feloniously, deliberately and of their malice aforethought and with premeditation and deliberation , shooting him, the said Oscar Chitwood on the head and body of him,the said Oscar Chitwood with a pistol which said pistol was then and there loaded with gun powder and leaden bullets,and was then and there had and held in their hands,of which wounds the said Oscar Chitwood did then and there die against the peace and dignity of the State of Arkansas.

And the Grand Jury aforesaid in the name and by the authority aforesaid further accuse the said John Rutherford of the crime of being accessory to the crime of murder in the first degree committed as folows,to-wit: One Ben Murray and others to the Grand Jurors unknown in the County of Garland,and state of Arkansas,on said 26th day of December,1910, did feloniously ,willfully and of their malice aforethought and with deliberation and premeditation kill and murder one Oscar Chitwood by then and there willfully , feloniously ,deliberately and of their malice aforethought and with premeditation and deliberation shooting him,the said Oscar Chitwood on the body and head of him,the said Oscar Chitwood,with a pistol then and there held in their hands,and which said pistol was then and there.loaded with gun powder and leaden bullets,of which wounds the said Oscar Chitwood did then and there die and the said John Rutherford was then and there present ,standing by and willfully ,feloniously,deliberately and of his malice aforethought and with premeditation and deliberation ,aiding ,abetting and assisting in the act of said killing and murder

Both counts of this indictment being for one and the same offense

against the peace and dignity of the State of Arkansas.

[signature]
Prosecuting Attorney.

Indictment of John Rutherford. *Courtesy of Garland County Courthouse.*

prisoners escape.[303] Sheriffs across the state paid particular attention to this charge and worried that it might create a legal precedent that would limit their freedom to house prisoners as they thought best.[304] The grand jury also indicted Sid Houpt on two counts of "non-feasance in office" because he did not comply with Judge Evans's orders to search suspected gambling houses in the county and destroy illegal gambling equipment. The grand jury's remaining fifteen indictments were levied against other defendants allegedly involved in illegal gambling in Hot Springs.[305]

Judge Calvin Cotham allowed Sid Houpt to post bail but removed him from office pending trial, throwing the sheriff's office into chaos once again. With nobody left in the sheriff's office whom the county courts trusted,

Cotham appointed local businessman Charles Webb as Garland County sheriff. Webb was Garland County's third sheriff in little more than three months. Locals described Webb as "one of the leaders in the reform movement," who took a moderate position by promising to enforce the law against gambling while also opposing a law against Sunday baseball games proposed by radical reformers in the county.[306] Within hours of taking office, Webb raided illegal gambling clubs, seizing and publicly burning much of the gambling equipment the grand jury indicted Sid Houpt for refusing to find and destroy.[307]

After the grand jury announced the indictments of Murray and Rutherford, Hot Springs mayor W.W. Waters asked Sheriff Webb to remove Murray and Rutherford from the city jail and keep them in the county jail, since he had "no desire for the city government of Hot Springs to mix in any manner with the government of the county of Garland." Across the state, Webb's comments sparked conversations as people wondered if Waters was disdainful of the corruption in Garland County's government or if he was worried that someone might break into the city jail to kill the two men.[308] It is not entirely clear what Waters was thinking, but the mayor had good reasons to worry that someone might try to murder Rutherford and Murray.[309]

John Rutherford's trial began with jury selection on May 22, 1911. J.B. Wood presented the state's case with help from James L. Graham, who was also representing the Chitwood family in a wrongful death suit against members of the sheriff's department.[310] Colonel George Murphy led Rutherford's defense team.[311] As is often the case with high-profile cases, it was difficult to find an impartial jury, since most members of the community had already made up their minds.[312] After a contentious selection process, the court empaneled a jury, but several days into the trial, J.B. Wood discovered that R.L. Gilliam, a good friend of Sid Houpt and John Rutherford, had accompanied deputy sheriff Bailey when Bailey summoned jurors. Wood argued that Gilliam had "controlled the actions" of Bailey during the juror-summoning process and, thus, corrupted the jury. Wood urged the court to throw out the jury and select a new jury. The court refused Wood's petition, and the case proceeded.[313]

J.B. Wood presented the prosecution's case that numerous witness statements proved conclusively that John Rutherford conspired with Ben Murray to murder Oscar Chitwood and make it look like a lynching. The prosecution's case rested primarily on two groups of witnesses. People living near the courthouse testified that no lynch mob could have possibly left the courthouse grounds undetected, which contradicted Rutherford's claims that such a mob murdered Chitwood. The defense knew that the prosecution's case relied heavily on prisoners who were in the Garland County jail the night of Chitwood's death, so in a stunning last-minute move, George Murphy presented a motion to the court that would have prevented the prisoners who had been convicted of crimes from taking the stand. The court might have been surprised, but J.B. Wood was not. He responded to the defense motion with a document from Governor Donaghey that pardoned all the former prisoners who testified for the state. The pardon came "as a distinct surprise to the defendant's counsel."[314] The prisoners testified that they heard Oscar Chitwood beg "Mr. Houpt" not to kill him and that they saw Rutherford and Murray murder Chitwood.[315] Jack Purnell, awaiting trial for murder the night of Chitwood's death, testified that while the deputies typically allowed the prisoners to keep their windows open at night, on the night of Chitwood's murder, Ben Murray demanded that the prisoners keep the windows closed. When one prisoner opened his window anyway, "Murray cursed him severely." Purnell also testified that the night Chitwood died was "the first night that the negro women were locked in their cells." On every other night before that, deputies allowed the women to enjoy the "run around" of the jail.[316]

George Murphy presented the defense's counterargument that Rutherford was a dedicated public servant who felt no personal animosity toward Oscar Chitwood and did everything short of sacrificing his own life to protect Chitwood from the lynch mob.[317] Most of the defense witnesses either testified to John Rutherford's good character or argued that the prosecution's witnesses were untrustworthy.[318] Since the prosecution relied primarily on witnesses who were prisoners in the county jail, it was easy to argue that those witnesses were both untrustworthy in general and that they may have felt animosity toward members of law enforcement, like Rutherford. It does not appear that Murphy produced a single witness other than Rutherford to testify that they saw a lynch mob. Sid Houpt's testimony for the defense was as focused on proving his own innocence as on defending Rutherford, arguing that his family played no part in any conspiracy since they all wanted a public trial, which, he argued, would conclusively vindicate them from all suspicions of wrongdoing and celebrate Jake Houpt's memory.[319] John Rutherford took the stand in his own defense to provide his version of the murder and to suggest that J.B. Wood and other anti-gambling leaders in Garland County were prosecuting Rutherford in an effort to remove the Houpt family from power. On cross-examination, Rutherford admitted that the Houpt family was paying his legal fees, although he argued this was proof that the Houpts were dedicated to protecting innocent public servants like himself and not because they wanted to influence his testimony or protect their own interests.[320]

The courtroom was packed with an audience that sweltered in the nearly unbearable spring heat, but no one dared make a sound or leave for fear that they might miss some shocking development. Prosecution and defense lawyers battled viciously in a series of objections and counter objections that stopped just short of physical violence. Local legal analysts believed that while Rutherford's lawyers were putting up an impressive fight, J.B. Wood was presenting a much stronger case for the prosecution. A guilty verdict seemed inevitable.[321]

At 11:20 a.m. on May 31, 1911, the court clerk read the verdict: "We the jury find John Rutherford not guilty of the murder of Oscar Chitwood."[322] The courtroom erupted into noise as Rutherford rushed to the jury box, where he shook hands with each juror and thanked them all profusely. Rutherford informed reporters that he was pleased, but not surprised, by the verdict, since he "did not see how an unprejudiced jury could do otherwise than acquit." Prosecuting attorney J.B. Wood declined to comment on the case as he left the courthouse.[323]

Rutherford's murder trial was over, but other cases growing out of the Chitwood murder followed.

James L. Graham, who helped Wood with the prosecution and who represented Chitwood's family in a wrongful death suit against Rutherford, Murray and Sid Houpt, expressed his intention to continue the lawsuit. He believed that he could win the lawsuit despite Rutherford's acquittal because civil suits required a lesser burden of proof than criminal cases.[324] When the Chitwood family struggled to pay Graham's legal fees, people from all over Arkansas donated money to support the family's lawsuits.[325] Graham eventually won a $150,000 judgement against Houpt for the Chitwood family, but Garland County judge Calvin Cotham later set aside the judgement on procedural grounds.[326]

J.B. Wood continued to fight what he argued was corruption in Garland County. In June 1911, he obtained grand jury indictments against two members of the Rutherford jury for illegally passing out liquor in the jury room. However, the grand jury found no evidence that any member of the jury engaged in any illegal attempts to influence the outcome of the trial.[327] The same grand jury found that former Garland County sheriffs Robert L. Williams, Jake Houpt and Sid Houpt had mishandled a combined total of $2,376.97 in county funds. Judge Thurston Farmer announced that if

INDICTMENT.

STATE OF ARKANSAS,
Against
Sid Houpt

Garland Circuit Court
INDICTMENT.

The Grand Jury of Garland County, in the name and by the authority of the State of Arkansas, accuse Sid Houpt of the crime of non-feasance in office committed as follows: The said Sid Houpt in the County and State aforesaid, on the 21st day of March A. D., 1911 was then and there sheriff of said Garland County and a warrant was duly issued and directed by W.H.Evans, Judge of the Circuit Court of said Garland County, then and there having been placed in his hands as such sheriff directing and commanding him as such sheriff to make search at 336 1/2 Central Avenue over the Ohio Club Bar in the City of Hot Springs, in the County of Garland and State of Arkansas for certain gambling devices commonly called faro bank, roulette, klondike and crap tables and that if said gambling devices be found then that he as such sheriff forthwith proceed publicly to burn the same according to law; which said gambling devices were then and there being unlawfully set up and exhibited at said place contrary to the statute in such case made and provided, the said Sid Houpt as such sheriff as aforesaid then and there having said warrant in his hands which had been duly issued and delivered to him as aforesaid and it then and there being his duty to make search at said place for said gambling devices and if found to forthwith proceed publicly to burn the same according to law and as directed by said warrant, did unlawfully and willfully omit, fail, refuse and neglect to make search at said place for said gambling devices and to seize and burn the same according to law and as directed by said warrant; contrary to his duty as such sheriff and against the peace and dignity of the State of Arkansas.

J.P. Hoad
Prosecuting Attorney.

Indictment of Sid Houpt. *Courtesy of Garland County Courthouse.*

the money was not repaid by the third Monday of July, he would pursue charges.[328] In September 1911, J.B. Wood obtained additional indictments against officials, including the recently appointed Garland County sheriff Charles Webb, who, the grand jury found, had not done enough to fight illegal gambling in the county.[329]

After a long legal battle, a Garland County jury convicted Sid Houpt of allowing Rutherford and Murray to escape from jail. The court fined him one dollar and sentenced him to one hour in jail. The sentence was light, but the conviction permanently removed him from office.[330] Houpt appealed his conviction to the Arkansas Supreme Court, arguing that while he did allow Rutherford and Murray to leave the jail, they remained within his effective control and that, as sheriff, the law allowed him some flexibility in how he maintained control of prisoners. The Arkansas Supreme Court disagreed with Houpt's argument, found that the lower courts had applied the law correctly and upheld Houpt's conviction.[331] Sid Houpt returned to his family's property in the countryside, where he worked primarily as a farmer until his death in 1937, when he was laid to rest in the family plot near his brother Jake.[332]

Despite the public outcry against Oscar Chitwood's murder, nobody was ever held responsible for his death. Rutherford was found not guilty. It appears he returned to the family farm and lived a peaceful life.[333] Ben Murray was released and never put on trial for Chitwood's murder but remained a "shadowy Hot Springs character" who was involved in bootlegging, auto theft and even conspiring to murder a federal official with a charge of, yes, nitroglycerin, for which he was sentenced to fifteen years in prison.[334] The mysterious "unknown" other conspirators mentioned in the coroner's jury proceedings and in the grand jury indictments were never officially named or brought to trial. The Houpt family retreated from public life, and in the century that has passed since Sid Houpt's removal from office, no member of the Houpt family has held office in the county government that they once dominated.

Rutherford was never convicted of murder in a court of law, but surviving historical evidence leaves little doubt that he murdered Oscar Chitwood. His motives are less clear. Chitwood's family lawyer, James L. Graham, argued that Rutherford and Murray conspired with the Houpt family to murder Chitwood as an act of vengeance for the death of Jake Houpt.[335] Graham's theory might be the most obvious explanation, but it is not the only one. Rutherford might have acted alone. Rutherford and Chitwood knew each other, and the deputy might have felt understandable personal animosity for the man he believed was responsible for murdering the popular sheriff. Rutherford might have invented the lynching story to give the appearance of popular support for a deeply personal murder. If this theory is true, it is consistent with the findings of Christopher Waldrep, who argued that the Ku Klux Klan "designed their killings to resemble lynchings, hoping to win community support by making it look like they already had it."[336] It is also possible that Rutherford and Murray might have killed Chitwood, with or without the approval of the Houpts, in hopes of rehabilitating their personal reputations, which were damaged by their abortive attempt to claim the reward for Chitwood's capture. The two deputies might have believed that their claims that a lynch mob murdered Chitwood would shield them from criminal prosecution while the community thanked them behind closed doors. If that was their plan, it might have worked. The jury acquitted Rutherford despite overwhelming evidence of his guilt, and while many people condemned the murder in public, others might have thanked him in private.

Rutherford's acquittal was a major setback for reformers in Hot Springs. J.B. Wood did break the political power of the Houpt family, but Hot Springs remained the home of numerous illegal gambling dens until 1967, when Governor Winthrop Rockefeller sent in the state police to shut down criminal businesses in the city. Even Rockefeller's victories were limited and probably did more to encourage the legalization than the abolition of vice in the spa city. Today, Hot Springs remains a complicated city where millions of visitors from around the world gamble tens of millions of dollars at the largest casino and racetrack in the state, drink alcohol at the city's numerous bars, enjoy shows at euphemistically titled "gentlemen's clubs" and purchase marijuana at the largest dispensary in the region, all while remaining within walking distance of numerous churches that condemn those activities. Hot Springs, perhaps more than any other city in the South, provides a physical embodiment of the conflict between the praying South and the hedonistic South as described by Ted Ownby.[337]

Oscar Chitwood was not lynched. There is no doubt whatever about that, but his story demonstrates what can happen in a society that allows lynching. There is a strong antiauthoritarian strand of thought in the United States that rallies around the slogan that "the government should fear the people," but the story of Oscar Chitwood demonstrates the practical problems with that ideology. A government that fails to maintain a monopoly on violence becomes little more than an impotent spectator to anarchy. Oscar Chitwood was probably a criminal, and the people of Garland County had every right to hold Chitwood accountable for his actions. However, Oscar Chitwood was also a person, and under the Sixth Amendment to the Constitution, every person accused of a crime deserves a day in court. Oscar Chitwood died begging, "For God's sake don't kill me. Let me stand trial."[338] It was a powerful cry that echoes through the streets of every community that tolerated the "crime of the highest order."[339]

CHAPTER 6

CONCLUSION

The biblical texts describing how God hardens the heart of Pharaoh also hardens the heart of its readers, so they can later celebrate with no pangs of conscience the ten plagues God brought upon the Egyptians.

—*Adi Ophir,* The Order of Evils[340]

Oscar Chitwood was not lynched, but two other men, both of them African American, were murdered by mobs in Hot Springs in the coming years in a manner that typifies what we now call "spectacle" lynchings, carried out in full daylight in front of massive crowds of people.

On June 19, 1913, an African American man named Will Norman was lynched in downtown Hot Springs for having allegedly murdered fourteen-year-old Garland Huff, the daughter of prominent attorney C. Floyd Huff and a darling of local society. Garland Huff was murdered between ten and eleven o'clock on the morning of June 19, 1913, "as she battled off the advances of Will Norman," her father's servant, according to the *Arkansas Gazette*, but this was sheer speculation, with another local newspaper, the *Hot Springs New Era*, admitting that the only evidence against Norman was his flight from the scene of the crime.[341] Huff's skull was reportedly crushed in five places—the alleged murder weapon, a mallet, was reportedly lying nearby—and she was stuffed into a closet, hidden away until one of her brothers opened the closet around the noon hour, finding her. Physicians were summoned, and the girl was rushed to St. Joseph's Infirmary, where she died at seven that evening.

Thirty minutes after the discovery of the body, the *Sentinel-Record* had published a special edition that employed all the tropes of southern lynching culture. The newspaper described Norman as "the negro brute, whose bestial passion prompted the killing," while Garland Huff was presented as the heroic victim, almost presaging Flora Cameron in *The Birth of a Nation*, a movie that would be released two years later: "That the little girl foiled the outrage, and took death rather than suffer at the brute's hands, is indicated in the circumstances." As the *Sentinel-Record* relates it, Norman "evidently tried to rape the girl, and when she fought back, picked up a heavy potato mallet and beat her over the head with it. There are depressions in the forehead, and the skull is fractured in the back of the head." Twice in the brief piece did the newspaper comment on the likelihood of a lynching, writing the second time, "That there will be a lynching is very little doubted in the event the negro is captured alive. He has no connections here, having come from Alabama."[342]

According to the *Gazette*, as news of the event quickly spread, "crowds began to gather, armed in open manner, and the woods were honeycombed with grim-visaged men determined to seek out and find the brute and silently acquiescing in a general scheme to make short work of him when he was found."[343] The *Gazette* put the mob's size at three thousand men, while the *Democrat* estimated it at four thousand, the size of the mob being inflated by a large number of summertime visitors in Hot Springs, mostly coming from the South; "and these having little else to do in the afternoon," they participated in the pursuit of Norman.[344] The *Gazette*'s lengthier account of the mob's activities holds that large numbers of men were already hunting for Norman by the time word of the assault filtered to the Hot Springs business district, where "those who had remained in the city joined in the demand for the negro's life and from every door there appeared men and boys armed with rifles, revolvers and shotguns. Many negroes joined in the demand for weapons. A local sporting goods firm passed out every weapon in stock to the eager hands reaching for them. Thousands of rounds of ammunition were distributed."[345]

Two men named Tom McCafferty and Ernest Simms were credited with Norman's capture out on the road to Cedar Glades. The two vigilantes forced Norman into their buggy and drove him back to Hot Springs. Upon being informed by McCafferty that Garland Huff had died, Norman reportedly said to the two men, "Well, I am sorry. I suppose I will be dead, too, in a little while, and I deserve it." Upon arrival at the county jail, the two vigilantes discovered that the sheriff and deputies were still out on the search, and a group of five hundred men quickly surrounded the buggy and took Norman themselves. News reached the Huff family, and the *Gazette* records that, though he wanted to see Norman killed, C. Floyd Huff was prevailed upon to remain at home; he did, however, give his boys permission to attend the lynching after they asked, "Father, may we go see that negro lynched, please?" As the *Sentinel-Record* reported, "The negro was fairly booted north on Ouachita avenue to the triangular intersection of Ouachita and Central. The crowd wanted a conspicuous place. They did not want to merely hang the negro but to hang him where he would be seen by all, and under the glare of an electric light. The crowd moved speedily. Small boys joined in the program. They shouted and jeered the negro brute. Some kicked him." Apparently, in their haste to hang Norman, the crowd failed to note that McCafferty remained tied to him, and the latter man "had to extricate himself speedily not to be dragged along with him."[346]

At the intersection of Ouachita Avenue and Central Avenue, Norman was hanged from an electric light pole, and his body was riddled with bullets. After this murder, someone called out, "Let's burn him," and the body was cut down and "taken to a point within a short distance and thrown upon a pile of wood quickly arranged." Within a half hour, only bones remained.[347] By the following day, people were picking through the ashes of the fire, gathering bones and breaking them up into small pieces for souvenirs.[348] At the time, John W. Hildreth operated Hildreth's Restaurant at 202 Ouachita Avenue (the site of the future Como Hotel), while his wife, Jeannie, ran a grocery store at 207 Ouachita; they also oversaw a woodyard behind the restaurant. According to historian Inez Cline, "When the infamous lynching of June 1913 occurred, after hanging the man on a light pole located at the junction of Central and Ouachita, the mob used three cords of Mrs. Hildreth's wood to burn the body. Ashes were placed in 'penny' match boxes and sold as souvenirs."[349]

The next lynching took place on August 1, 1922. The victim was Gilbert Harris, nicknamed "Bunk" or "Punk," whose age was given as "about 28" by newspaper reports. Newspapers did not provide an occupation for Harris, though all the accounts emphasized that Harris reportedly had a long criminal career.[350] Records of the Arkansas Department of Correction (ADC) state that Gilbert Harris was sentenced to twelve years for grand larceny and burglary on October 30, 1917. The description of him in the ADC paperwork lists his age at the time of processing as twenty-three, his height as five feet, five inches and his occupation as "laborer." He had one prior conviction, he had completed the second grade and his mother, Edna

Lynching of Gilbert Harris. *Courtesy of the Garland County Historical Society.*

Stubbes, then thirty-eight years old, was still living. He was listed as married, though his wife's name was not given, and he was a user of tobacco.[351] Harris's inmate record contains a "Notice of Escape" that outlines how he managed to free himself: "This man was stationed at Camp #3, under Warden Nuckolls, he escaped last night through a window from the trusty quarters up stairs, his escape was discovered this morning."[352]

Harris was lynched for having allegedly murdered Maurice Connally, a twenty-six-year-old businessman heading the insurance department of the Arkansas Trust Company, who resided at the Scheweder apartments at 433 Orange Street.[353] Connally was also the nephew of county judge Charles H. Davis and a member of various fraternal organizations, as well as a veteran of World War I who had trained as an officer at Fort Roots in central Arkansas before being sent overseas.

According to newspaper accounts, Harris was in the act of burglarizing Connally's apartment when the businessman returned home around midnight from a dance at the Como Hotel.[354] The two men fought, and Harris, who was carrying a .45-caliber pistol, fired twice, hitting Connally once in the abdomen. Harris fled, while Connally was able to call out to his neighbors and was immediately taken to the hospital.[355] The initial *Hot Springs New Era* report contains two sentences that may give some clue as to why police zeroed in on Harris so quickly: "After the shooting the burglar ran from the front of the house and south on Woodbine street. He ran at a slow pace and seemed to look back to see if anyone was following. Several neighbors awakened by the shot saw the negro." About two hours after the shooting, Harris was arrested at his home by a group of four police officers that included Sid Houpt, currently serving as a deputy constable. Connally had apparently been able to describe his assailant to authorities, and officers reportedly found at Harris's home a .45-caliber pistol that had recently been fired (and fifteen shells for the gun), along with a pair of wet, dirty socks, which fit with Connally's statement that the man who shot him was in his stocking feet. Too, a cap found at Connally's place was identified by Harris's wife as belonging to her husband.[356] Harris reportedly admitted having committed a variety of robberies and petty thefts, including taking rings from the hands of a "young white girl…while she was asleep," but he denied any connection to the murder.[357]

A mob reportedly began gathering at the city jail around six in the morning on August 1. An hour later, Connally succumbed to his wound, and at the news of this, the mob grew hostile. According to the *Democrat*, by eight o'clock, the alley between the city hall building (which contained the jail) and the Business Men's League was "swarming with men and the street in front was well filled," with many discussing their plans for a lynching. Police Chief Oscar Sullivan had apparently taken measures to deal with possible mob violence, ordering the doors shut and barred; he also "ordered his men to prevent negroes from grouping and to search them when they insisted on doing so." Sullivan asked the newly arrived circuit judge Scott Wood to address the crowd, and he did, promising the assembled mass a special session of the court and a speedy trial. His request that the mob disperse went unheeded. Mayor Harry A. Jones asked those who were willing to leave Harris to the authorities to raise their hands—only two responded and were quickly booed.

The *Democrat* reported that mob members hoped their presence might spook the police into trying to move Harris to Little Rock for safekeeping, thus offering them an opportunity to snatch the alleged murderer. However, after some minutes went by without such action, the mob proceeded to break into the jail. As the *New Era* related it, one group went "down the stairs from the main floor of the building to the jail, which is in the basement," while another "gathered at the side door." When Sullivan and fellow officers came out of the cell block area, they "found themselves confronted on all sides by an array of guns. At the same time, the crowd on the outside battered down the side door and another group rushed in, their front ranks fairly bristling with revolvers."[358] These men easily outnumbered the local officers and succeeded in taking Harris from the custody of authorities. The mob placed Harris in a truck and drove him to the triangle in front of the Como Hotel, at the intersection of Ouachita and Central Avenues (the same place where Will Norman was murdered).[359] There, the noose was placed around his neck, and Harris was offered the chance to confess, but he protested his innocence instead, claiming that he was indeed at the Connally home but that "another negro" or "the old man" had done the shooting. According to the *Hot Springs New Era*, after this profession of innocence was rejected, "Harris was hoisted about 20 feet in the air while the great crowd yelled and cheered. He only lived a few minutes. The body was allowed to hang perhaps half an hour and then was let down. Negro undertakers came for the body, but the mob chased them away. Some of the more unruly members attempted to drag the body from the truck, intending to drag it through the streets, but cool heads prevailed and the body was carried up to the city jail, where it was locked up."[360]

An inquest held by the coroner, Dr. J.B. Shaw, returned the typical verdict of death "at the hands of unknown parties." In fact, the inquest was very

Hot Springs Confederate Memorial. *Courtesy of Christopher Thrasher.*

brief, with the only witnesses called being five members of law enforcement, including Sullivan and Sheriff W.R. Downen. Both testified to being outnumbered and outgunned by the mob but were apparently not asked if they could identify any of the individuals who participated in the lynching.[361]

The site where Norman and Harris were lynched became, on June 2, 1934, the location where the city's new Confederate monument was unveiled to the public. This monument depicts a soldier, in stone, standing with his hands gripping the barrel of a rifle, the butt of which rests on the ground by his foot. His equipment includes a bedroll, canteen and bullet pouch. The sculpture itself is six feet high, set on a base twelve feet high, making a very visible presence in the plaza overlooking Central, Ouachita, Market and Olive Streets in downtown Hot Springs. The north face of the base is inscribed "1861 / 1865 / CONFEDERATE SOLDIERS," while the south face acknowledges the organization that put this statue in place: "ERECTED / IN LOVING MEMORY / BY THE / HOT SPRINGS CHAPTER / UNITED DAUGHTERS / OF THE CONFEDERACY."[362] As Charles Russell Logan has written, "By 1934, Arkansas already was home to more than 30 Civil War monuments, including at least three honoring Union troops. Nationally the landscape was literally dotted with thousands of Civil War monuments. Yet, in 1934, almost 70 years after the war, Hot Springs was one of the last cities 'of size' in Arkansas without a marble or bronze Confederate 'soldier' in its downtown area."[363]

Although Hot Springs was perhaps tardy in its material commemoration of the Confederacy at a prominent downtown site, the city made up for it with the splendor of its celebration, which was headlined by Mayor Leo McLaughlin and featured performances of "Dixie," "The Star-Spangled Banner" and "Taps" by the high school band.[364] Today, a much newer, less sightly and oddly off-putting plastic sign near the monument informs visitors that this is "PRIVATE PROPERTY NO TRESSPASSING." The plastic sign reminds us that not everyone is welcome here.

Downtown Hot Springs has attracted the occasional demonstration by neo-Confederates, self-described patriots and others who have a propensity to wave the Confederate and Gadsden flags. Three such gatherings occurred in Hot Springs prior to August 19, 2017, and attracted little attention, consisting of a handful of people waving flags and being studiously ignored by tourists and locals alike. However, the August 19 event took place only a week after white supremacists murderously marched on Charlottesville, Virginia, and tensions were higher than usual in Hot Springs.[365] The counter-protestors outnumbered the demonstrators, and local officials said that the two groups combined accounted for 350–400 people at the peak, with only a few arrests made for disorderly conduct. *Arkansas Times* photographer Brian Chilson captured an African American woman marching down historic Central Avenue with a sign reading: "TWO BLACK MEN WERE LYNCHED WHERE YOUR CONFEDERATE MONUMENT STANDS."[366]

Following the murder of George Floyd in Minneapolis, Minnesota, by police officer Derek Chauvin on May 25, 2020, local opposition to the presence of the Confederate monument was again renewed, this time with at least one official, city manager Bill Burrough, expressing the desire that the statue be relocated, while also noting that the statue's location on private property, owned by the UDC, limited the city's options. As he told the *Sentinel-Record*, "I'm hoping to be able to meet with the United Daughters of the Confederacy's board and have a dialogue with them in reference to the monument," and although a petition drive for the relocation of the statue was underway, it could only reflect the temperament of its signers, not exert any influence upon the government.[367] However, a few days later, the *Sentinel-Record* reported that the UDC was "not interested in meeting at this time."[368] Later that month, a local attorney, Joshua Drake, proposed painting a "Black Lives Matter" mural on private property in the area around the statue.[369] By early July, however, momentum on the issue had stalled, with city manager Burrough noting that he had "more pressing concerns with the ongoing COVID-19 pandemic," adding that he needed more time to research the issues behind the possible relocation of the statue, including the possibility of exercising eminent domain over that piece of property.[370]

Irony abounds in this whole situation. The current revival of interest in the history of lynching has been driven, in large part, by outrage over police violence against African Americans, violence that, due to its distribution across the airwaves and social media, has replicated the spectacles of yore even if only a few individuals were in attendance at the actual event. As we have seen, the murder of George Floyd was the genesis of the most recent round of criticism against the Confederate monument in Hot Springs—a murder that recalled, for local residents, the history of the two lynchings that took place at the site of that monument. However, Hot Springs was also the site of a notorious murder perpetrated by members of the local police force, but memory of that particular killing has not been revived as we seek to draw parallels between the injustices of the past and the injustices of the present, despite this particular case being a most egregious example of police violence. After all, John Rutherford and Ben Murray did not kill Oscar Chitwood in the heat of the moment, when anger might well overcome judgement, or when training within a warrior culture overrides the basic requirement that officers, more than anything else, "keep the peace." Instead, they rid themselves of Chitwood in a most premeditated fashion, shooting down their helpless prisoner in the cold, dark hours of the day after Christmas.

No, Oscar Chitwood was not lynched, but what happened to him speaks to our present moment as much as do the thousands of lynchings of years gone by. We can see in his story how excessive charges could be laid on someone despite all evidence to the contrary; after all, George Chitwood shot the sheriff, but Oscar Chitwood was slated to stand trial for it—and possibly forfeit his life for something every witness agreed he did not do. No doubt many public defenders and advocates for the incarcerated could see here some parallels to their own work. We can see in his story how, when Oscar Chitwood was murdered, every news outlet unquestioningly parroted the information provided by those people assigned to protect him, and by the time doubts began to surface about this narrative, the national newspapers had moved on to other stories. No doubt many critics of our media could identify with that. And lastly, we can see in his story the brave work not only of attorneys but also of the witnesses who took the stand despite their unprivileged positions to testify to a truth that might put them in danger in such a corrupt and insular society and how all this dedication and courage led to naught the moment the jury returned to exonerate the man for something nearly every witness agreed he did, in fact, do. No doubt all of us who have followed similar trials these past years, whether of police officers or self-appointed vigilantes who see themselves acting in that role, have felt that same depth of disappointment and despair.

As anthropologist Gretchen E. Schafft has written, "As we strive to bring more information into the light, we recognize and respect the variability of human nature found in those victims and perpetrators who lived this history and realize that we are required, in the interest of truth, to be open to all the information we can gather."[371] That is what we have attempted to accomplish with this book—and why, we feel, it is important to ground analyses of violence in the history and culture of those localities where it occurred, for it is there where we find the variability of human nature. After all, the same class of people who carried out the two lynchings mentioned in this conclusion earlier threatened to rise in defense of black teenager Harry Poe in 1910, and the men and women who were angered at the murder of Sheriff Jake Houpt were also incensed at the cold-blooded and cowardly killing of Oscar Chitwood by the late sheriff's friends and colleagues. There are no easy or consistent patterns here. In his essay "In Defense of the Fragment," historian Gyanendra Pandey observes that the grand narratives social scientists produce "tend to be about 'context' alone, or at least primarily: the larger forces of history that tend to produce violent conflicts."[372] Here, we have aimed, instead, to tell a smaller story that highlights the variability of local decision-making, for good or ill. Where that Confederate statue in Hot Springs tries to render complex history into flat heritage, we assert that we are not condemned to honor the slavers and lynchers and murderers of our past—we have an array of ancestors from which to choose, all of them gloriously complex individuals.

Until we can tell the stories of men who were not lynched, like Oscar Chitwood, alongside the stories of the men who were, like Will Norman and Gilbert Harris, we shall continue to have an incomplete picture of the past and thus remain ignorant of the ways in which societies were regulated and lives destroyed beyond the actions of the mob. The past, for those who want to make this world better, has utility. We can take events that have happened and map them onto the present as a means of better understanding what is going on right now and why, and with that understanding, we can perhaps better plan how to prevent or combat the same evils that visited our forebears.

The story of lynching alone does not tell us enough to aid us in the present struggle against police violence and vigilantism. We also need the story of people like Oscar Chitwood, who was not lynched but who, nevertheless, ended up like so many victims of the mob—just another bloody corpse on the courthouse grounds.

NOTES

Chapter 2

1. For statements regarding Hot Springs as so-called neutral ground, see: Francis J. Scully, *Hot Springs, Arkansas and Hot Springs National Park: The Story of a City and the Nation's Health Resort* (Little Rock, AR: Pioneer Press, 1966), 5; Dee Brown, *The American Spa: Hot Springs, Arkansas* (Little Rock, AR: Rose Publishing, 1982), 9.
2. Bobbie Jones McLane, Charles William Cunning and Wendy Bradley Richter, comps., *Observations of Arkansas: The 1824–1863 Letters of Hiram Abiff Whittington* (Hot Springs, AR: Garland County Historical Society, 1997), 69.
3. Mark Blaeuer, *Didn't All the Indians Come Here? Separating Fact from Fiction at Hot Springs National Park* (Fort Washington, PA: Eastern National, 2007), 6.
4. Mary Beth Trubitt, "'Archaic Arkansas'—The Jones Mill Archeological Project," Arkansas Archeological Survey, accessed July 3, 2021, https://archeology.uark.edu/learn-discover/current-research/archaic-arkansas/.
5. Blaeuer, *Didn't All the Indians Come Here?*, 8.
6. Ibid., 11.
7. Ibid., 29–37.
8. Ibid., 45–48.
9. Thomas A. Chambers, *Drinking the Waters: Creating an American Leisure Class at Nineteenth-Century Mineral Springs* (Washington, D.C.: Smithsonian Institution Press, 2002), 34; quoted in Blaeuer, *Didn't All the Indians Come Here?*, 50.

10. Blaeuer, *Didn't All the Indians Come Here?*, 59.
11. Ibid., 50.
12. Ibid., 27.
13. "Thousands of Artifacts Archived in Bath House," *Sentinel-Record* (Hot Springs, AR), July 1, 2014.
14. Charles Hudson, *Knights of Spain, Warriors of the Sun: Hernando de Soto and the South's Ancient Chiefdoms* (Athens: University of Georgia Press, 1997), 317–18.
15. Ann M. Early, "Finding the Middle Passage: The Spanish Journey from the Swamplands to Caddo Country," in *The Expedition of Hernando de Soto West of the Mississippi, 1541–1543: Proceedings of the De Soto Symposia 1988 and 1990*, ed. Gloria A. Young and Michael P. Hoffman (Fayetteville: University of Arkansas Press, 1993), 69.
16. Trey Berry, "'Amongst the Greatest Natural Curiosities in the Country': Dunbar and Hunter at the Hot Springs, 1804–1805," *Record* (Garland County Historical Society, 2004): 23. See also Trey Berry, Pam Beasley and Jeanne Clements, eds., *The Forgotten Expedition: The Louisiana Purchase Journals of Dunbar and Hunter, 1804–1805* (Baton Rouge: Louisiana State University Press, 2006).
17. Sharon Shugart, "What's a Nice Set of Springs Like You Doing in a Place Like This? The Bathhouses at the Hot Springs of Arkansas: 1809–1878," *Record* (Garland County Historical Society, 2013): 3.4–3.5.
18. For more information on these particular travelers, see Andrew J. Milson, *Arkansas Travelers: Geographies of Exploration and Perception, 1804–1834* (Fayetteville: University of Arkansas Press, 2019).
19. Ruth Irene Jones, "Hot Springs: Ante-Bellum Watering Place," *Arkansas Historical Quarterly* 14 (Spring 1955): 3–31; Ray Hanley, *A Place Apart: A Pictorial History of Hot Springs* (Fayetteville: University of Arkansas Press, 2011), 5–11; Shugart, "Nice Set of Springs," 3.4–3.6.
20. Sharon Shugart, "What's in a Claim? The Litigious History of the Ouachita Hot Springs," *Record* (Garland County Historical Society, 2012): 22–26.
21. Regina A. Bates, "'Our Long Lost Patrimony': The Belding Family's Battle for the Spa, 1849–1887 (master's thesis, Arkansas Tech University, 2014), 1–3; Shugart, "What's in a Claim?," 39–42.
22. Walter L. Brown, "The Henry M. Rector Claim to the Hot Springs of Arkansas," *Arkansas Historical Quarterly* 15 (Winter 1956): 281.
23. Brown, "Henry M. Rector Claim," 283; Shugart, "What's in a Claim?" 27–36.

24. Bates, "Our Long Lost Patrimony," 5; Shugart, "What's in a Claim?" 37–39.
25. Brown, "Henry M. Rector Claim," 284.
26. Bates, "Our Long Lost Patrimony," 6–7.
27. Ibid., 9–10.
28. Shugart, "What's in a Claim?" 45.
29. Ibid., 47.
30. Bobbie Jones McLane, "1860 Hot Spring County, Arkansas, Slave Schedule Summary," *Record* (Garland County Historical Society, 1991): 50–51.
31. Bates, "Our Long Lost Patrimony," 7–8.
32. Isabel Anthony, ed., *Garland County, Arkansas: Our History and Heritage* (Hot Springs, AR: Garland County Historical Society, 2009), 93, 300; Dorothy Lockhart Logan, "A History of Black Education in Hot Springs Prior to Integration," *Record* (Garland County Historical Society, 1976): 63.
33. Wendy Richter, "The Impact of the Civil War on Hot Springs, Arkansas," *Arkansas Historical Quarterly* 43 (Summer 1984): 128–30; Wendy Richter, "150 Years Ago: A 'Capital' Time at the Spa," *Record* (Garland County Historical Society, 2012): 58.
34. Francis J. Scully, *Hot Springs, Arkansas, and Hot Springs National Park: The Story of a City and the Nation's Health Resort* (Little Rock, AR: Pioneer Press, 1966), 47.
35. Wendy Bradley Richter and Inez Halsell Cline, *They Can't Go Home: A History of Northwestern Garland County, Arkansas, Including the Towns of Buckville and Cedar Glades* (N.p.: 1990), 24–25.
36. Tom DeBlack, *With Fire and Sword: Arkansas, 1861–1874* (Fayetteville: University of Arkansas Press, 2003), 31.
37. Frank Arey, "The Skirmish at McGrew's Mill," *Clark County Historical Journal* (2000): 63–66; DeBlack, *With Fire and Sword*, 77.
38. *War of the Rebellion: Official Records of the Union and Confederate Armies*, series 1, vol. 22, part 1 (Washington, D.C.: Government Printing Office, 1888), 753.
39. Richter, "Impact of the Civil War," 141.
40. Mary D. Hudgins, interview with Joe Golden, in *Bearing Witness: Memories of Arkansas Slavery: Narratives from the 1930s WPA Collections*, 2nd ed., ed. George E. Lankford (Fayetteville: University of Arkansas Press, 2006), 158–61.
41. Anthony, *Garland County, Arkansas*, 96; Mamie Ruth (Stranburg) Abernathy, "History of Hot Springs Special School District No. 6

of Garland County, 1881–1985," *Record* (Garland County Historical Society,1985): 81–83.
42. Gail Payton Spears, "African Americans and the Hot Springs Baths," *Record* (Garland County Historical Society, 2007): 24.
43. James Byrd, "African Americans and the Bathhouses of Hot Springs, Arkansas," *Record* (Garland County Historical Society, 2018): 5.6, 5.7.
44. Spears, "African Americans," 26.
45. Linda McDowell, "Jackson D. Page," *Record* (Garland County Historical Society, 2008): 167–70.
46. Orval E. Allbritton, *Dangerous Visitors: The Lawless Era* (Hot Springs, AR: Garland County Historical Society, 2008), 13.
47. Allbritton, *Dangerous Visitors*, 14–17.
48. Ibid., 25–28.
49. Orval E. Allbritton, *Leo and Verne: The Spa's Heyday* (Hot Springs, AR: Garland County Historical Society, 2003), 4.
50. Ann L. Greene, "The Arlington Hotel: An Arkansas Institution, 1875–1945," *Record* (Garland County Historical Society, 1996): 3.
51. Greene, "Arlington Hotel," 6.
52. "In Ashes," *Arkansas Gazette* (Little Rock, AR), March 6, 1878; "A Helping Hand," *Arkansas Gazette*, March 8, 1878.
53. Sharon Shugart, "Hot Springs National Park," in *Garland County, Arkansas: Our History and Heritage* (Hot Springs, AR: Garland County Historical Society, 2009), 348.
54. Allbritton, *Leo and Verne*, 5.
55. Ibid., 14; untitled, *Southern Standard* (Arkadelphia, AR), November 17, 1877; "Local Paragraphs," *Arkansas Gazette*, September 25, 1879.
56. Allbritton, *Leo and Verne*, 14–15; "Shot in the Street," *Arkansas Gazette*, September 23, 1882; "Col. S. W. Fordyce's Vindication," *Arkansas Gazette*, April 1, 1884.
57. "Colonel S. W. Fordyce," *Arkansas Gazette*, August 5, 1919.
58. "A Ride to Death," *Arkansas Gazette*, February 10, 1884. See also "Flynn-Doran," *Arkansas Gazette*, February 17, 1884.
59. Allbritton, *Leo and Verne*, 15, 18; "Saturday's Slaughter," *Arkansas Gazette*, February 12, 1884; untitled editorial, *Arkansas Gazette*, February 12, 1884.
60. "Hot Springs," *Arkansas Gazette*, February 14, 1884; "Hot Springs," *Arkansas Democrat* (Little Rock, AR), February 26, 1884.
61. "Flynn-Doran," *Arkansas Democrat*, February 19, 1884.
62. "Hot Springs," *Arkansas Democrat*, February 21, 1884.

63. Untitled, *Osceola Times*, May 3, 1884; "Hot Springs," *Arkansas Democrat*, May 13, 1884.
64. "Flynn-Doran," *Arkansas Democrat*, March 29, 1886. For a personal account of the whole affair, see Mary D. Hudgins, "The Flynn-Doran Battle," *Record* (Garland County Historical Society, 1973): 41–63.
65. "Shot Down," *Arkansas Gazette*, July 19, 1887; "Our Specials," *Arkansas Gazette*, July 23, 1887; "Our State Specials," *Arkansas Gazette*, July 27, 1887.
66. Allbritton, *Leo and Verne*, 23.
67. "Hot Spring Central Avenue Historic District," National Register of Historic Places nomination form; on file at Arkansas Historic Preservation Program, Little Rock, AR; online at http://www.arkansaspreservation.com/ (accessed April 27, 2022); Allbritton, *Leo and Verne*, 61.
68. "Five Men Shot to Death; Pandemonium at Hot Springs," *Arkansas Gazette*, March 17, 1899.
69. Orval Allbritton, "A City Drenched in Blood," *Record* (Garland County Historical Society, 1996): 23.
70. Allbritton, "City Drenched in Blood," 26.
71. "Calm after Storm," *Arkansas Democrat*, March 18, 1899.
72. Allbritton, "City Drenched in Blood," 34.
73. Ibid., 36.
74. Elliot G. Bowen, "Mecca of the American Syphilitic: Doctors, Patients, and Disease Identity in Hot Springs, Arkansas, 1890–1940" (PhD diss., State University of New York at Binghamton, 2013), 60–61.
75. Ibid., 63–65.
76. Fred Cron, "Hot Springs' Military Hospital: The Army and Navy Opened One Hundred Years Ago," *Record* (Garland County Historical Society, 1987): 83.
77. Cron, "Hot Springs' Military Hospital," 87.
78. Kathryn Blair Carpenter, "Access to Nature, Access to Health: The Government Free Bathhouse at Hot Springs National Park, 1887 to 1922" (master's thesis, University of Missouri–Kansas City, 2019); Sharon Shugart, "The Legacy of Ral City," *Record* (Garland County Historical Society) 2008: 62–75; Stacey S. Eley, "A Look at the Origins and Challenges of the Government Free Bath House, 1878–1922," *Record* (Garland County Historical Society) 1997: 95–101.
79. Bowen, "Mecca of the American Syphilitic," 3.

80. Ibid., 11.
81. Charles Rosenberg, "Pathologies of Progress: The Idea of Civilization as Risk," *Bulletin of the History of Medicine* 72.4 (1998), 714–30; quoted in Bowen, "Mecca of the American Syphilitic," 12.
82. Bowen, "Mecca of the American Syphilitic," 42.
83. Ibid., 86, 130–33; Janis Kent Percefull, "The USPHS Venereal Disease Clinic at Hot Springs, Arkansas: Director O.C. Wenger's Legal Angle," *Record* (Garland County Historical Society, 2004): 32–51; Janis K. Percefull, "Wayward Girls/Hard Boiled Sisters of Arkansas: Their Incarceration and Medical Treatment in the Early Twentieth Century," *Record* (Garland County Historical Society, 2008): 120–29.
84. Mary D. Hudgins, "The Drumming Evil," *Record* (Garland County Historical Society, 1977): 89.
85. Ibid., 92.
86. Ibid., "Drumming Evil," 93.
87. Quoted in Dan Duren, *Boiling out at the Springs: A History of Major League Baseball Spring Training at Hot Springs, Arkansas* (Dallas, TX: Hodge Printing, 2006), 23.
88. Ibid., 43.
89. Ibid., 88.
90. Allbritton, *Leo and Verne*, 176.
91. "Opening Day of Hot Springs Races," *Arkansas Gazette*, February 26, 1904.
92. Oaklawn almost failed to open due to an attempt to burn down the grandstand; the identity of the perpetrator was unknown. Then bad weather scuttled the inaugural event. See "Attempt to Burn Down Grandstand," *Arkansas Gazette*, February 12, 1905; "No Opening at Oaklawn Track," *Arkansas Gazette*, February 14, 1905; "One Favorite Won at Oaklawn," *Arkansas Gazette*, February 16, 1905.
93. Allbritton, *Leo and Verne*, 178–79.
94. "Amis Anti-Racing Bill Special Order Monday," *Arkansas Gazette*, February 1, 1907; "Amis Bill Signed by Gov. J.I. Moore," *Arkansas Gazette*, February 28, 1907.
95. "Oaklawn Fight in Acute Stage Now," *Arkansas Gazette*, March 5, 1907.
96. Isabel Burton Anthony, "Happy Birthday Oaklawn Jockey Club: Oaklawn Park Celebrates a Century of Thoroughbred Racing," *Record* (Garland County Historical Society, 2004): 4.
97. "Citizens Move against Oaklawn," *Arkansas Gazette*, March 9, 1907; "Oaklawn Will Close Meeting," *Arkansas Gazette*, March 28, 1907.

98. Christopher Thrasher, "Hot Springs Fire of 1905," CALS Encyclopedia of Arkansas, accessed July 1, 2021, https://encyclopediaofarkansas.net/entries/hot-springs-fire-of-1905-12570/; Allbritton, *Leo and Verne*, 27–29.
99. "$1,250,000 Lost by Great Fire at Hot Springs," *Arkansas Gazette*, February 26, 1905; "Officials Think Great Fire Was Work of Firebugs," *Arkansas Gazette*, February 28, 1905.
100. Mike Shinn, "Garland County Courthouse," National Register of Historic Places nomination form, on file at Arkansas Historic Preservation Program, Little Rock, Arkansas; online at http://www.arkansaspreservation.com/ (accessed April 27, 2022).
101. "Negro Brute Attempts an Assault on School Girl," *Sentinel-Record* (Hot Springs, AR), January 26, 1910.
102. The sources disagree about the date of several events of this story of Harry Poe. For example, the article "Harry Poe Forfeited His Life on the Gallows," *Hot Springs (AR) Daily News*, September 2, 1910, states that the incident took place on January 28. Other sources, such as "Negro Must Hang at Hot Springs on April 1," *Arkansas Democrat*, March 2, 1910, state that the incident took place on January 18. While many sources, including many of the legal documents preserved by the Garland County Courthouse, state that Adams was attacked on January 28, the first available newspaper account of the attack (dated January 26) states that the attack took place on January 25. This appears to be the most likely date of the attack.
103. "Negro Brute Attempts an Assault on School Girl," *Sentinel-Record*, January 26, 1910.
104. Ibid.
105. Ibid.
106. "Police Have Dog and Cap," *Sentinel-Record*, January 27, 1910.
107. Ibid.
108. "Posse Out After Harry Poe," *Arkansas Gazette*, January 27, 1910.
109. "Negro Brute May Escape," *Sentinel-Record*, January 28, 1910.
110. "Harry Poe Forfeited His Life," *Hot Springs (AR) Daily News*, September 2, 1910.
111. "Negro Brute," *Sentinel-Record*, January 28, 1910.
112. "Negro Is Rushed to Little Rock," *Arkansas Gazette*, January 29, 1910; "Negro Is Spirited Away," *Arkansas Gazette*, February 1, 1910.
113. "Try Negro at Special Term," *Sentinel-Record*, January 29, 1910.

114. "Negro Is Rushed," *Arkansas Gazette*, January 29, 1910; "Negro Is Spirited Away," *Arkansas Gazette*, February 1, 1910.
115. "Try Negro," *Sentinel-Record*, January 29, 1910.
116. Ibid.
117. Guy Lancaster, *American Atrocity: The Types of Violence in Lynching* (Fayetteville: University of Arkansas Press, 2021), 43–70.
118. Preliminary hearing, *State of Arkansas v. Harry Poe*, Garland County Courthouse, Hot Springs, AR.
119. Motion for new trial, *State of Arkansas v. Harry Poe*, Garland County Courthouse, Hot Springs, AR.
120. Preliminary hearing, *State of Arkansas v. Harry Poe*, Garland County Courthouse, Hot Springs, AR.
121. Ibid.
122. "Negro Must Hang at Hot Springs on April 1," *Arkansas Democrat*, March 2, 1910.
123. "Tuck Negro Under Seat," *Sentinel-Record*, February 1, 1910.
124. Preliminary hearing, *State of Arkansas v. Harry Poe*, Garland County Courthouse, Hot Springs, AR.
125. "Tuck Negro Under Seat," *Sentinel-Record*, February 1, 1910.
126. "Change of Venue Cause of Threat," *Sentinel-Record*, February 5, 1910.
127. Ibid.
128. "Special Court to Convict Poe," *Sentinel-Record*, February 5, 1910.
129. "Change of Venue," *Sentinel-Record*, February 5, 1910.
130. "Poe Face Penalty," *Sentinel-Record*, February 26, 1910.
131. "Makes Appeal for the Law," *Sentinel-Record*, February 5, 1910.
132. Indictment, *State of Arkansas v. Harry Poe*, Garland County Courthouse, Hot Springs, AR.
133. "Negro Must Hang," *Arkansas Democrat*, March 2, 1910.
134. Motion for new trial, *State of Arkansas v. Harry Poe*, Garland County Courthouse, Hot Springs, AR.
135. "Decisions of Supreme Court," *Arkansas Gazette*, May 10, 1910.
136. "Two Weeks Given for Brief in Poe Case," *Arkansas Gazette*, May 22, 1910; "Decision of the Supreme Court," *Arkansas Gazette*, June 7, 1910; "Negro Stoically Awaits His Death," *Arkansas Gazette*, July 21, 1910.
137. "Plead for Harry Poe," *Sentinel-Record*, June 16, 1910.
138. "Citizens Warn Poe's Council," *Arkansas Gazette*, July 28, 1910.
139. "Negro Pays Death Penalty," *Batesville (AR) Guard*, September 9, 1910.
140. "Will Send Militia to Attend Poe's Hanging," *Arkansas Gazette*, August 11, 1910.

141. "County Prisoners Testify in Secret at Chitwood Inquest," *Sentinel-Record*, December 29, 1910.
142. "Asks Stay of Execution," *Arkansas Gazette*, August 31, 1910.
143. "Negro Pays Death Penalty," *Batesville Guard*, September 9, 1910.
144. "Harry Poe Forfeited His Life," *Hot Springs Daily News*, September 2, 1910.

Chapter 3

145. "Chitwood Makes Statement," *Sentinel-Record*, August 21, 1910.
146. Orval E. Allbritton, *Hot Springs Gunsmoke* (Hot Springs, AR: Garland County Historical Society, 2006), 150.
147. "Rutherford and Murray Were Taken into Custody," *Arkansas Democrat*, December 29, 1910; Allbritton, *Leo and Verne*, 51.
148. Allbriton, *Leo and Vern*, 46.
149. Ibid.
150. "In Fusillade with Mountaineer," *Sentinel-Record*, August 18, 1910.
151. Ibid.
152. United States Census for 1900, Lincoln Township, Garland County, AR, 167a.
153. "Sheriff Houpt Mortally Wounded," *Arkansas Gazette*, August 18, 1910.
154. Convict Registers, vols. 1998/038-138–1998/038-176. Texas Department of Criminal Justice. Archives and Information Services Division, Texas State Library and Archives Commission, Austin, TX.
155. "In Fusillade with Mountaineer," *Sentinel-Record*, August 18, 1910.
156. "Sheriff Houpt Mortally Wounded," *Arkansas Gazette*, August 18, 1910.
157. Ted Ownby, *Subduing Satan: Religion, Recreation, and Manhood in the Rural South, 1865–1920* (Chapel Hill: University of North Carolina Press, 2014), 1.
158. *State of Arkansas v. Sid Houpt*, March 21, 1911, Garland County Courthouse Archives; Allbritton, *Leo and Verne*, 51.
159. "Chitwood Makes Statement," *Sentinel-Record*, August 21, 1910.
160. "In Fusillade with Mountaineer," *Sentinel-Record*, August 18, 1910.
161. Allbriton, *Hot Springs Gunsmoke*, 151.
162. "In Fusillade with Mountaineer," *Sentinel-Record*, August 18, 1910.
163. Allbriton, *Hot Springs Gunsmoke*, 151.

164. "In Fusillade with Mountaineer," *Sentinel-Record*, August 18, 1910.
165. Allbriton, *Hot Springs Gunsmoke*, 153.
166. "Hot Chitwood without Bond," *Sentinel-Record*, August 25, 1910.
167. Ibid.
168. Allbriton, *Hot Springs Gunsmoke*, 153.
169. "In Fusillade with Mountaineer," *Sentinel-Record*, August 18, 1910.
170. Ibid.
171. Allbriton, *Hot Springs Gunsmoke*, 153.
172. "Houpt Rallies during Night," *Sentinel-Record*, August 19, 1910.
173. Ibid.
174. Allbriton, *Hot Springs Gunsmoke*, 153.
175. "In Fusillade with Mountaineer," *Sentinel-Record*, August 18, 1910.
176. Ibid.
177. Bryan J. Vila and Gregory J. Morrison, "Biological Limits to Police Combat Handgun Shooting Accuracy," *American Journal of Police* (1994), 10; online at https://s3.wp.wsu.edu/uploads/sites/208/2016/08/Biological-Limits-to-Police-Combat-Handgun-Shooting-Accuracy.pdf.
178. "In Fusillade with Mountaineer," *Sentinel-Record*, August 18, 1910.
179. Allbriton, *Hot Springs Gunsmoke*, 155.
180. "In Fusillade with Mountaineer," *Sentinel-Record*, August 18, 1910.
181. Ibid.; *City Directory for Hot Springs, Arkansas*, 1910, 190. Accessed at the Garland County Historical Society.
182. "Houpt Rallies during Night," *Sentinel-Record*, August 19, 1910.
183. U.S. Department of Labor, Union Scale of Wages and Hours of Labor 1907 to 1912, 37. Available at https://fraser.stlouisfed.org/title/union-scale-wages-hours-labor-3912/union-scale-wages-hours-labor-1907-1912-476865.
184. "In Fusillade with Mountaineer," *Sentinel-Record*, August 18, 1910.
185. "Houpt Rallies during Night," *Sentinel-Record*, August 19, 1910.
186. "Oscar Chitwood Surrenders," *Sentinel-Record*, August 20, 1910.
187. Ibid.
188. "Sheriff Jake Houpt Passes Away," *Sentinel-Record*, August 21, 1910.
189. "Masons Conducted Funeral," *Sentinel-Record*, August 23, 1910.
190. "Resolution to Houpt Memory," *Sentinel-Record*, August 25, 1910.
191. "Sheriff Houpt Is Dead from Wound." *Arkansas Gazette*, August 21, 1910.
192. "Chitwood Makes Statement," *Sentinel-Record*, August 21, 1910.
193. Ibid.
194. Ibid.

195. Ibid.
196. Ibid.
197. "Chitwood Will Not Lose Arm," *Sentinel-Record*, August 23, 1910.
198. "Oscar Chitwood Held for Murder," *Arkansas Gazette*, August 25, 1910.
199. "Hear Chitwood Petition Monday," *Arkansas Gazette*, December 10, 1910.
200. "Hot Chitwood without Bond," *Sentinel-Record*, August 25, 1910.
201. "Oscar Chitwood Held," *Arkansas Gazette*, August 25, 1910.
202. "Chitwood Involved in Stolen Horse Trade," *Arkansas Gazette*, August 27, 1910.
203. "Sid Houpt Is Appointed," *Sentinel-Record*, August 23, 1910.
204. "Commission Goes to Sid Houpt as Sheriff," *Arkansas Democrat*, August 22, 1910.
205. Grady McWhiney and Forrest McDonald, *Cracker Culture: Celtic Ways in the Old South* (Tuscaloosa: University of Alabama Press, 2012), 148.
206. "Commission Goes to Sid Houpt," *Arkansas Democrat*, August 22, 1910.
207. Allbriton, *Hot Springs Gunsmoke*, 156.
208. "Not Entitled to the Reward," *Sentinel-Record*, September 11, 1910.
209. "Suit Filed Over Chitwood Reward," *Sentinel-Record*, August 23, 1910.
210. "Will Remove Chitwood in Few Days," *Arkansas Gazette*, September 8, 1910.
211. "Looking After Chitwood," *Arkansas Democrat*, September 26, 1910.
212. "Sheriff Houpt Is Dead from Wound." *Arkansas Gazette*, August 21, 1910.
213. "Chitwood Is Indicted for Murder of Houpt," *Arkansas Gazette*, November 10, 1910.
214. "Hears Court Warrant Read," *Arkansas Democrat*, November 16, 1910.
215. "Chitwood Is Taken to Hot Springs," *Pine Bluff (AR) Daily Graphic*, December 8, 1910.
216. "Hear Chitwood Petition Monday," *Arkansas Gazette*, December 10, 1910.
217. "Change of Venue Granted," *Arkansas Gazette*, December 16, 1910.
218. "Oscar Chitwood Shot and Killed by Men," *Sentinel-Record*, December 27, 1910.
219. "Chitwood Riddled with Bullets by Mob," *Arkansas Democrat*, December 26, 1910.
220. "Did One Man or a Mob Kill Chitwood?" *Arkansas Democrat*, December 28, 1910.
221. "Chitwood Riddled with Bullets," *Arkansas Democrat*, December 26, 1910.

222. Ibid.
223. Ibid.
224. "Rutherford and Murray Were Taken into Custody," *Arkansas Democrat*, December 29, 1910.
225. "Sid Houpt in Little Rock," *Arkansas Gazette*, December 31, 1910.
226. "Oscar Chitwood Shot," *Sentinel-Record*, December 27, 1910.
227. "Chitwood Riddled with Bullets," *Arkansas Democrat*, December 26, 1910.
228. "Oscar Chitwood White Murderer," *Vicksburg (MS) Evening Post*, December 26, 1910.
229. "Arkansas Mob Riddles Body," *Chattanooga (TN) News*, December 26, 1910.
230. "Mob Takes Prisoner from Deputy," *Butte (MT) Daily Post*, December 26, 1910.
231. "Mob Shoots Man Dead," *Tacoma (AZ) Times*, December 26, 1910.

Chapter 4

232. Ashraf H.A. Rushdy, *The End of American Lynching* (New Brunswick, NJ: Rutgers University Press, 2012), 8.
233. Ken Gonzales-Day, *Lynching in the West, 1850–1935* (Durham, NC: Duke University Press, 2006).
234. See the chart at Brent E. Riffel, "Lynching," CALS Encyclopedia of Arkansas, https://encyclopediaofarkansas.net/entries/lynching-346/ (accessed April 29, 2022). All of the Arkansas lynchings mentioned in this chapter have separate entries in the CALS Encyclopedia of Arkansas.
235. Brent M.S. Campney, "State Studies and the Whiteness of White-on-White Lynching," *Journal of the Gilded Age and Progressive Era* 20 (January 2021): 110.
236. Ibid., 111.
237. "State News," *Arkansas Gazette*, January 25, 1871.
238. "State News," *Arkansas Gazette*, February 4, 1872; "State News," *Arkansas Gazette*, May 31, 1872.
239. "Lynch Law: Three Horse Thieves Hung in Sarber County," *Arkansas Gazette*, August 8, 1874; "Facts About the Hanging at Roseville," *Western Independent (Fort Smith, AR)*, August 13, 1874; "Franklin County: About Clayton's Outrage Mill—The Lynching of the Harris Boys," *Arkansas Gazette*, November 7, 1874.

240. "State News—Polk," *Arkansas Gazette*, August 11, 1877.
241. "Arkansas Justice," *Arkansas Gazette*, October 29, 1878.
242. "Judge Lynch at Work," *Arkansas Gazette*, March 16, 1879.
243. "Lynch Law," *Arkansas Gazette*, May 28, 1879.
244. Richard Maxwell Brown, *Strain of Violence: Historical Studies of American Violence and Vigilantism* (New York: Oxford University Press, 1975), vii.
245. Brown, *Strain of Violence*, 93.
246. Lynn Strawberry, "'Protect the Innocent and Bring the Guilty to Justice': The Anti-Horse Thief Association in Western Arkansas" (master's thesis, University of Arkansas, 1995), 24–24, 36–37; "Good Work Has Been Done," *Springdale* (AR) *Twice-a-Week News*, April 27, 1909.
247. "Anti-Horse Thief Men in Session," *Arkansas Gazette*, October 10, 1915.
248. Strawberry, "Protect the Innocent," 66.
249. "Lynched," *Arkansas Democrat*, May 21, 1892; "To a Finish," *Arkansas Gazette*, May 22, 1892.
250. "Town Marshal Shot," *Arkansas Gazette*, March 22, 1901; "To a Bridge," *Arkansas Gazette*, March 24, 1901.
251. "Cox's Murderer Lynched at Brinkley," *Forrest City (AR) Times*, November 9, 1903; "Assassin of J.C. Cox Taken from Jail by Mob, Lynched at Brinkley," *Arkansas Democrat*, November 10, 1903; "White Man Shot to Death by Mob," *Arkansas Gazette*, November 10, 1903; "Lynching at Brinkley," *Forrest City Times*, November 13, 1903; "Cut His Throat," *Forrest City Times*, November 13, 1903.
252. Richard S. Daniels, "Blind Tigers and Blind Justice: The Arkansas Raid on Island 37, Tennessee," *Arkansas Historical Quarterly* 38 (Autumn 1979): 259–70.
253. "Sheriff Mauldin Dies in Discharge of Duty," *Osceola (AR) Times*, August 6, 1915; "Our Martyr," *Osceola Times*, August 6, 1915.
254. "Mauldin's Murderer Died in Cell Tuesday," *Osceola Times*, August 13, 1915.
255. Amy Kate Bailey and Stewart E. Tolnay, *Lynched: The Victims of Southern Mob Violence* (Chapel Hill: University of North Carolina Press, 2015), 201.
256. "Mother and Child Shot to Death," *Arkansas Gazette*, December 28, 1904; "An Awful Deed Committed," *Arkansas Democrat*, December 28, 1904.
257. "Efforts to Solve Murder Mystery," *Arkansas Gazette*, December 30, 1904.

258. "Father and Son Held for Murder," *Arkansas Gazette*, December 31, 1904.
259. "Mob at Newport Lynch White Man," *Arkansas Gazette*, January 1, 1905.
260. "The Newport Lynching," *Arkansas Gazette*, January 3, 1905.
261. "Death at Hands of Unknown Mob," *Arkansas Gazette*, January 4, 1905.
262. Untitled editorial, *Arkansas Gazette*, January 5, 1905.
263. "A Diabolical Deed," *Arkansas Gazette*, May 21, 1887; "Judge Lynch," *Arkansas Gazette*, May 22, 1887; "Judge Lynch," *Arkansas Democrat*, May 30, 1887.
264. "D.S. Thud," *Arkansas Gazette*, May 14, 1892.
265. "He's Gone: No Longer Will the Lecherous Beast Indulge His Lust upon Earth," *Arkansas Gazette*, May 14, 1892. For a fuller account, read Guy Lancaster, "Before John Carter: Lynching and Mob Violence in Pulaski County, 1882–1906," in *Bullets and Fire: Lynching and Authority in Arkansas, 1840–1950*, ed. Guy Lancaster (Fayetteville: University of Arkansas Press, 2018), 170–77.
266. Karlos Hill, *Beyond the Rope: The Impact of Lynching on Black Culture and Memory* (New York: Cambridge University Press, 2016), 54.
267. Jeannie Whayne, "Henry Lowery Lynching: A Legacy of the Elaine Massacre?" in *Race, Labor, and Violence in the Delta: Essays to Mark the Centennial of the Elaine Massacre*, ed. Michael Pierce and Calvin White Jr. (Fayetteville: University of Arkansas Press, 2022), 73.

Chapter 5

268. "Stirring Up Strife," *Arkansas Democrat*, December 27, 1910.
269. "County Prisoners Testify in Secret at Chitwood Inquest," *Sentinel-Record*, December 29, 1910.
270. "Did One Man or a Mob Kill Chitwood?" *Arkansas Democrat*, December 28, 1910.
271. "County Prisoners Testify in Secret," *Sentinel-Record*, December 29, 1910.
272. Ibid.
273. "One Man or a Mob?" *Arkansas Democrat*, December 28, 1910.
274. "Sensational Developments in the Chitwood Inquest," *Sentinel-Record*, December 28, 1910.

275. "One Man or a Mob?" *Arkansas Democrat*, December 28, 1910.
276. "County Prisoners Testify in Secret," *Sentinel-Record*, December 29, 1910.
277. "One Man or a Mob?" *Arkansas Democrat*, December 28, 1910.
278. "Andy Chitwood Reported Dying," *Sentinel-Record*, December 28, 1910.
279. "County Prisoners Testify in Secret," *Sentinel-Record*, December 29, 1910.
280. "Who Was Third Man in Chitwood Case?" *Arkansas Democrat*, January 4, 1911.
281. "Rutherford and Murray Were Taken into Custody," *Arkansas Democrat*, December 29, 1910.
282. "Houpt Arrives Home," *Arkansas Democrat*, December 31, 1910.
283. "Chitwood Riddled with Bullets," *Arkansas Democrat*, December 26, 1910.
284. "One Man or a Mob?" *Arkansas Democrat*, December 28, 1910.
285. "Stirring Up Strife," *Arkansas Democrat*, December 27, 1910.
286. "The St. Louis Times Says," *Arkansas Democrat*, December 29, 1910.
287. "The Killing of a Prisoner of the Law," *Arkansas Gazette*, December 28, 1910.
288. "Murder Condemned," *Sentinel-Record*, December 30, 1910.
289. "St. Louis Times Says," *Arkansas Democrat*, December 29, 1910.
290. "Deputies Give Their Version," *Sentinel-Record*, January 2, 1911.
291. "In Fusillade with Mountaineer," *Sentinel-Record*, August 18, 1910.
292. "One Man or a Mob?" *Arkansas Democrat*, December 28, 1910.
293. "Deputies Give Their Version," *Sentinel-Record*, January 2, 1911.
294. "Bail Hearing for Accused," *Pine Bluff Daily Graphic*, March 7, 1911.
295. "Deputies Held Responsible in Chitwood Case," *Arkansas Gazette*, January 3, 1911.
296. "Murray and Rutherford," *Sentinel-Record*, January 19, 1911.
297. "Deputies Are Denied Bail," *Arkansas Gazette*, February 1, 1911.
298. "City Will Keep the Prisoners," *Sentinel-Record*, March 1, 1911.
299. "Both Deputies Were Indicted," *Pine Bluff Daily Graphic*, April 16, 1911.
300. "Indictment," *State of Arkansas v. John Rutherford*, Garland County Courthouse, Hot Springs, AR.
301. "Both Deputies Were Indicted," *Pine Bluff Daily Graphic*, April 16, 1911.
302. "Rutherford and Murray Indicted," *Arkansas Gazette*, April 16, 1911.

303. "Indictment," *State of Arkansas v. Sid Houpt*, Garland County Courthouse, Hot Springs, AR.
304. "Rutherford and Murray Indicted," *Arkansas Gazette*, April 16, 1911.
305. "Both Deputies Were Indicted," *Pine Bluff Daily Graphic*, April 16, 1911.
306. "Houpt Is Removed from His Office," *Arkansas Gazette*, April 5, 1911.
307. "New Sheriff in His First Raid," *Arkansas Gazette*, April 15, 1911.
308. "Webb Asked to Move the Indicted Officers," *Arkansas Democrat*, April 22, 1911.
309. "Rutherford and Murray Were Taken into Custody," *Arkansas Democrat*, December 29, 1910.
310. "Nine of Twelve Jurors Selected," *Arkansas Gazette*, May 24, 1911.
311. "Jury Selected in Rutherford Case," *Arkansas Gazette*, May 25, 1911.
312. "Nine of Twelve Jurors," *Arkansas Gazette*, May 24, 1911.
313. "Motion to Quash Jury Selection," *State of Arkansas v. John Rutherford*, Garland County Courthouse, Hot Springs, AR.
314. "Governor Pardons State Witnesses," *Arkansas Gazette*, May 27, 1911
315. "July Selected," *Arkansas Gazette*, May 25, 1911.
316. "Rutherford Trial Is On in Earnest," *Arkansas Gazette*, May 26, 1911.
317. "July Selected," *Arkansas Gazette*, May 25, 1911.
318. "Witnesses for Defense," *State of Arkansas v. John Rutherford*, Garland County Courthouse, Hot Springs, AR.
319. "Denies Any Conspiracy," *Sentinel-Record*, May 27, 1911.
320. "Rutherford Relates Story of Killing," *Sentinel-Record*, May 28, 1911.
321. "State's Case Made Strong," *Sentinel-Record*, May 26, 1911.
322. "Jury Holds Rutherford Not Guilty of Murder of Oscar Chitwood," *Arkansas Democrat*, May 31, 1911.
323. "Rutherford Freed at Hands of Jury," *Arkansas Gazette*, June 1, 1911.
324. Ibid.
325. "Plan Second Suit against Officers," *Arkansas Gazette*, March 6, 1911.
326. "Big Judgement Set Aside," *Arkansas Gazette*, July 2, 1911.
327. "Two of Rutherford Jury Are Indicted," *Arkansas Gazette*, June 7, 1911.
328. "Former Sheriffs' Alleged Shortage," *Arkansas Gazette*, June 27, 1911.
329. "Indict Officials at Hot Springs," *Arkansas Democrat*, September 25, 1911.
330. "Sheriff Houpt Must Serve Sentence," *Arkansas Democrat*, October 23, 1911.
331. William M. McKinney and H. Noyes Greene, *The American and English Annotated Cases*, 692.

332. United States Census for 1930, accessed at https://www.familysearch.org/search/collection/1810731; Arkansas Death Record Index, 1670, accessed at https://digitalheritage.arkansas.gov/death-records-index-eg/.
333. United States Census for 1920, Garland County, Arkansas, accessed at https://www.familysearch.org/search/collection/1488411.
334. Allbriton, *Hot Springs Gunsmoke*, 151.
335. "Stirring Up Strife," *Arkansas Democrat*, December 27, 1910.
336. Christopher Waldrep, *The Many Faces of Judge Lynch: Extralegal Violence and Punishment in America* (New York: Palgrave Macmillan, 2002), 72.
337. Ted Ownby, *Subduing Satan: Religion, Recreation, and Manhood in the Rural South, 1865–1920* (Chapel Hill: University of North Carolina Press, 2014), 1.
338. "Who Was Third Man in Chitwood Case?" *Arkansas Democrat*, January 4, 1911.
339. "Stirring Up Strife," *Arkansas Democrat*, December 27, 1910.

Chapter 6

340. Adi Ophir, *The Order of Evils: Toward an Ontology of Morals*, trans. Rela Mazali and Havi Carel (New York: Zone Books, 2005), 345 (section 7.122).
341. "Negro Assailant of Girl Lynched," *Arkansas Gazette*, June 20, 1913; "Garland Huff Thought to Have Been Assaulted by Negro Boy," *Hot Springs (AR) New Era*, June 19, 1913. According to this report, Garland Huff had been left at the house with her grandmother and Norman, and her grandmother departed around 10:00 a.m. Huff's body was discovered at 11:00 a.m. Interestingly, this initial report in the *New Era* added the detail that Huff's clothing had been torn without adding an assumption of sexual assault. An extra edition, published later that day after Huff had died, repeats the paragraph about the thin evidence of the accusations against Norman.
342. "Daughter of Judge Huff Victim of Deadly Assault by Black," *Sentinel-Record*, June 19, 1913.
343. "Negro Assailant," *Arkansas Gazette*, June 20, 1913.
344. "Hot Springs Quiet After Awful Tragedy," *Arkansas Democrat*, June 20, 1913.
345. "Negro Assailant," *Arkansas Gazette*, June 20, 1913.

346. "Defending Her Chastity from Black Brute Miss Garland Huff Is Murdered," *Sentinel-Record*, June 20, 1913. There was later a petition circulated to raise money to reward McCafferty for his leading role in the capture of Norman. See "To Reward M'Cafferty for Capturing Norman," *Hot Springs New Era*, June 24, 1913.
347. According to the *Democrat* and the *Hot Springs New Era*, the body remained hanging for about an hour before it was cut down and burned. See "Hot Springs Quiet After Awful Tragedy," *Arkansas Democrat*, June 20, 1913; "Funeral of Garland Huff to Be Held Tomorrow at 2:30 O'Clock," *Hot Springs New Era*, June 20, 1913. The latter newspaper also reported that the coroner was then undecided as to whether he would hold an inquest or not.
348. "Judge Deplores Lynching of Negro," *Arkansas Gazette*, June 21, 1913.
349. Inez Cline, "Hotel Como: A Man and a Dream," *Record* (Garland County Historical Society, 1977): 2.
350. "Mob Hangs Spa Negro," *Arkansas Democrat*, August 1, 1922; "Negro Lynched by Hot Springs Mob," *Arkansas Gazette*, August 2, 1922; "Inquest Held Over Remains of Harris," *Hot Springs New Era*, August 1, 1922 (regular edition).
351. Gilbert Harris inmate record (ADC #15622), Arkansas Department of Correction, Pine Bluff, AR.
352. Notice of escape, Gilbert Harris inmate record (ADC #15622), Arkansas Department of Correction, Pine Bluff, AR.
353. News reports of the time spell his name as Connelly, and the initial *Gazette* report gives his age as thirty, but both the U.S. Census of 1910 and his tombstone render his name as Connally, and the census reports that he was born in 1896. He is recorded in the 1910 Census as living on Orange Street in Ward 1 of Hot Springs with mother, Ellen Chareder; stepfather N.H. Chareder; sister Marion (or Marian, as it is rendered in the 1920 Census); and several boarders.
354. The Como Hotel, or Hotel Como, was built in two sections in 1915–16 by Edward Hoadley Johnson. The name is derived from the first letter of the streets around the block: Central, Ouachita, Market and Olive. See Cline, "Hotel Como," 1–7.
355. Statewide sources differ on his destination, with the *Democrat* reporting that it was the New Park Hospital, while the *Gazette* identified the hospital as St. Joseph's Infirmary. However, the *Sentinel-Record* of Hot Springs, in an issue published before Connelly succumbed to his wound, reported his destination as the Park Hospital. See "Maurice

Conley Is Shot through Abdomen by Negro," *Sentinel-Record*, August 1, 1922.

356. "Negro Lynched," *Hot Springs New Era*, August 1, 1922 (extra edition); "Inquest Held," *Hot Springs New Era*, August 1, 1922; "Maurice Connelly Killed, Negro Lynched," *Hot Springs New Era*, August 1, 1922 (regular edition); "2 Negroes Lynched by Mobs in the South," *New York Times*, August 2, 1922.

357. "Connelly Slayer Taken from Jail, Hanged to a Post," *Sentinel-Record*, August 2, 1922.

358. "Negro Lynched," *Hot Springs New Era*, August 1, 1922 (extra edition).

359. According to the *Sentinel-Record* report on the lynching, an anonymous person first yelled, "Let's go to the woods," but another voice answered, "Como Square, that's the place." See "Connelly Slayer Taken from Jail," *Sentinel-Record*, August 2, 1922.

360. "Negro Lynched," *Hot Springs New Era*, August 1, 1922 (extra edition); "Mob Hangs Spa Negro," *Arkansas Democrat*, August 1, 1922; "Connelly Slayer Taken from Jail," *Sentinel-Record*, August 2, 1922; "Negro Lynched by Hot Springs Mob," *Arkansas Gazette*, August 2, 1922.

361. "Inquest Held," *Hot Springs New Era*, August 1, 1922 (regular edition).

362. John Slater, "Hot Springs Confederate Monument." National Register of Historic Places nomination form, on file at Arkansas Historic Preservation Program, Little Rock, AR; online at http://www.arkansaspreservation.com/ (accessed April 29, 2022).

363. Charles Russell Logan, *"Something So Dim It Must Be Holy": Civil War Commemorative Sculpture in Arkansas, 1886–1934* (Little Rock: Arkansas Historic Preservation Program, 1996), 4; online at http://www.arkansaspreservation.com/ (accessed April 29, 2022).

364. "Confederate Park Monument Will Be Unveiled Saturday," *Sentinel-Record*, June 2, 1934; "Monuments to Confederates Unveiled Here," *Sentinel-Record*, June 3, 1934.

365. Max Bryan, "Demonstration Planned Over Confederate Monuments," *Sentinel-Record*, August 18, 2017; Max Gregory, "Officials Take Steps to Protect Citizens, Private Property," *Sentinel-Record*, August 19, 2017; David Showers, "UDC Chapter Lowers Flag out of Caution," *Sentinel-Record*, August 19, 2017; Jacob Rosenberg, "Confederate Rally in Hot Springs Largely Peaceful, Met by Larger Counter-Protest," *Arkansas Blog*, August 20, 2017, https://www.arktimes.com/ArkansasBlog/archives/2017/08/20/confederate-rally-in-hot-springs-largely-peaceful-met-by-larger-counter-protest (accessed

April 29, 2022); Max Bryan, "Mostly Peaceful Crowd Turns Out for Demonstration," *Sentinel-Record*, August 20, 2017; Grace Brown, "Clergy Prays for Peace," *Sentinel-Record*, August 20, 2017.

366. Max Brantley, "When Johnny Reb Comes Marching to Hot Springs," *Arkansas Blog*, August 19, 2017, https://www.arktimes.com/ArkansasBlog/archives/2017/08/19/when-johnny-reb-comes-marching-to-hot-springs (accessed April 29, 2022).
367. Cassidy Kendall, "Statue Should Move, CM Says," *Sentinel-Record*, June 6, 2020.
368. Cassidy Kendall, "City Stalls on Confederate Statue Relocation," *Sentinel-Record*, June 9, 2020; Cassidy Kendall, "No Plans to Relocate Statue, UDC Spokesman Says," *Sentinel-Record*, June 12, 2020.
369. Cassidy Kendall, "'Black Lives Matter' Mural Proposed for Area around Statue," *Sentinel-Record*, June 27, 2020.
370. Cassidy Kendall, "Pandemic a Priority Over Statue, City Says," *Sentinel-Record*, July 4, 2020.
371. Gretchen E. Schafft, *From Racism to Genocide: Anthropology in the Third Reich* (Urbana: University of Illinois Press, 2007), 255.
372. Gyanendra Pandey, "In Defense of the Fragment: Writing about Hindu-Muslim Riots in India Today," *Representations* 37 (Winter 1992): 41.

INDEX

M

N

O

P

R

S

T

W

ABOUT THE AUTHORS

Christopher Thrasher earned his doctorate in American history from Texas Tech University. He currently serves as the director of the honors program and as an associate professor of history at National Park College in Hot Springs, Arkansas. In 2015, Thrasher published his first book, *Fight Sports and American Masculinity: Salvation in Violence from 1607 to the Present.* He published his second book, *Suffering in the Army of Tennessee: A Social History of the Confederate Army of the Heartland from the Battles for Atlanta to the Retreat from Nashville*, in 2021.

Guy Lancaster holds a PhD in heritage studies from Arkansas State University and currently serves as the editor of the online Encyclopedia of Arkansas, a project of the Central Arkansas Library System. He has authored, coauthored or edited several books on the history of violence in Arkansas, including *American Atrocity: The Types of Violence in Lynching* (2021).